Wise Eyes

SEE YOUR WAY TO SUCCESS

Christine Beckwith

20/20 VISION PRESS

Wise Eyes/ Christine Beckwith—1st edition.

20/20 Vision Press, an imprint of Manifest Publishing

ISBN 13: 978-1-944913-35-9

Contents

DEDICATION

I dedicate this book to my son Jagger, who has taught me that it is never too late to do something exceptional; that with focus and determination I can be both a great leader and mom, both a professional and a woman; that I can be proud of all I am.

You have raised my bar of self-expectation born out of desire to leave a legacy you will be proud of. You have saved my life literally and figuratively. One day, you will understand how. Thank you for helping me find the balance in my life and for bringing me the greatest joy and deepest love.

Due to the richness of our love and your existence in my life, I have a newfound quality of living that is unprecedented for me. You have helped me find a relentless source of inner motivation, which unlocked the core of my creativity and set the wheels of my dreams in motion, like writing this book.

In case you didn't already know, you are my world. Thank you for the inspiration!

FOREWORD

When Christine asked us to write the foreword for her book, we were surprised, and confused. We wondered, *"What would we say? Why would our accomplished middle child want us to write the foreword for her book?"* After all, people who write forewords are experts and highly educated. We said no. We told Christine we are not celebrities; we're ordinary people and suggested that she ask one of the famous people she knows.

And then, Christine being Christine, she taught us—her proud parents—a simple lesson: she would honor the people who, outside of herself, contributed the most to her book.

Thank you, Christine, for giving us this honor. We knew you would succeed in life. You were an exceptionally determined little girl. Making friends in school came easily and you still have some of those same friends today. You always got good grades and when you joined something, like sports or student council or cheerleading, you gave all out and never quit.

As parents, we encouraged you to go after whatever you decided to do. And you always went after it 100%. That is how you still are today.

We are proud of you, Christine—because you are our daughter, of course. And even more because you have done so much all on your own. We have watched you work hard to get to where you are today. You have climbed the ladder and traveled the world on your own abilities. And now you are Vice President of a national company. We always knew you could do this.

Christine, you have worked many years to write this book. We are pleased that your time and dedication has paid off and that your determination to finish has never wavered. This book was always on your mind and is a desire you've spoken of often.

One thing we know for certain about our daughter Christine is that when she decides to do something, she sees it through to the end. Christine can accomplish anything she puts her mind to. We are proud to be the parents of Christine Stiles Beckwith.

Merle and Sandy Stiles

Merle and Sandra Stiles are natives of New Hampshire who raised their family of three daughters in Meredith, NH. They met as teenagers and both worked in Meredith's Amatex Mill for nearly two decades until the mill's closing when they both took jobs at Aavid Engineering for another two decades. Both have since retired, however Merle continues to work part time for Parks and Recreation of Laconia, NH.

Merle and Sandra are hardworking, dedicated and loyal people. They epitomize and represent a generation of Americans who made this country great by doing their part to get up every day and help their community factories build and grow. The Stiles raised their daughters with a strong moral upbringing and they faithfully attended the local Advent Christian Church with their daughters while raising them.

Merle

Merle, the oldest child of a large family of eight, has a reputation for being patient and soft spoken. He is a man of wise words who sincerely loves people and would do anything for anybody. He believes in people and has taught his daughters to do the same and to put their faith in God.

Sandra

Sandy retired when she fell tragically ill from a brain aneurysm. She has since fully recovered and now spends her days caring for the family home. She is a salt of the earth *say it like it is* New Englander, who is extremely loyal, hardworking and dedicated to Merle and her daughters. If you want an honest opinion, you just need to ask Sandra and you will get one.

Christine is the culmination of both their personalities—her father's patience and love of people and her mother's thick skin and authentic speaker who can be relied on for genuine advice.

Together Merle and Sandy raised their three girls starting during their own teenage years while literally growing up themselves. They provided a warm and loving home for their daughters and always supported the dreams and life-choices their girls pursued.

In 2018 they will celebrate their 50th Anniversary, another fine example and testament to the wonderful people they are.

What if?

WHAT IF YOU HAD EYES FOR ALL THINGS that bring you success? What if you had a keen sense of focus on the priorities that render you the best return?

When I was a little girl, I was told we learn from mistakes in two ways: making your own mistakes or choosing to avoid mistakes by seeing the lesson taught in other's mistakes. *Wise Eyes: See Your Way to Success* will sharpen your sense of success sight and guide you to learn from my mistakes.

After that early advice, I became an insatiable student who kept notes and journals detailing my journey to professional success, always intending to use my own (and other's) real-life stories of triumph and tribulations to advance my goals and to help others.

The stories that punctuate this book reflect insights that have propelled my career over statistic defying odds to reach unfathomable levels of success. This is my life's story in a short, prioritized book spanning four decades. It is real and raw and brutally honest.

This book is also highly educational. It is my hope you will see the truth in the professional stories shared and use the lessons to shape your life; that you will draw upon the emotion of this shared life-experience to propel learning and absorb lessons.

I see, interact, and understand the world best through analogy. By contrasting and comparing experiences and events, life-lessons become our gateway to a better, stronger future. Over the course of the three sections of this book:

Section One: The Vision,

Section Two: The Action,

Section Three: The Mindset,

you will create your own future plan, build the skills and tools that allow you to enact your plan, and make the mental commitment necessary to ensure the future you see becomes your reality.

Wise Eyes: See Your Way to Success is your handbook to gain perfect eyesight and focus, enabling your walk along a direct path to incredible success.

This book has taken twists and turns along the way and very nearly never happened. I wrote it first more than a decade ago and put it away. It wasn't the right time and in truth I was not certain I would ever come back to it. Serendipity has brought people and circumstances into alignment and I am pleased to have unpacked the manuscript, blown the dust off the pages, and brought this book to you.

In thinking of a person or people to write the foreword, I realized my parents are the two people in my entire life who have had the greatest impact on me. My mother and father have overcome incredible odds both in terms of life accomplishment and financially. Despite the predictions and likelihood of failure, these two people whose own youth was cut short by parenting needs, succeeded in raising three children in a warm and loving home, while maintaining a keen work ethic and digging themselves out of a hole stemming from their start in life. They also defied marriage statistics and will celebrate their 50th anniversary in 2018.

In my genetics and inherent character, and in the learned behavior and moral core I rely on, lies the heritage of these two people who have shown determination and steadfast belief that, despite the odds, they would prevail.

It is appropriate my parents introduce this book. My story begins with them, and in their foreword, they say to the world why I am who I am today.

I hope this book inspires people. I write it to bring courage to those who have self-doubt or insecurity.

In these pages, I want to motivate those who believe there truly are no odds that can deter you when you set your mind to a goal and who accept there are no hurdles too high to overcome.

I hope everyone who takes the time to read my stories, my sales tips, and my professional advice will use this shared knowledge to create their own faster, smoother path to success.

Most of all, I hope you recognize your power. Even though there will be people in your journey who will want to slow you down, embarrass you, make you insecure, and create self-doubt, you have the power and ability to prevent their noise from diverting your path.

We all have greatness in us. It is up to you to nurture and harvest your greatness and to take each step, one after another, to propel yourself down your road to success. Everything in life is out there waiting for you to come and get it!

The Vision

Do you have a plan for your life? For your career? For your business? All plans start and end with vision—your vision. What do you see?

In this section, the focus is on having a plan, a vision, and executing it. Many people strive to succeed in life with no real understanding of how to get to their goals. Having an actionable Vision requires more than a carrot dangling in front of you.

I am fortunate to have learned early on how to nurture this vision and by sharing the techniques I've developed, I hope to ensure that you achieve the life to which you aspire and that you march through life towards measurable and tangible dreams, whatever they are!

"To dream is to allow oneself the ability to transcend to a better place, to imagine a better future. To then chase those dreams with a genuine belief that they can become a reality takes courage, strength, endurance, and some strategic ignorance. Lucky for me that is how I was born."

~C. B.

CHAPTER ONE

20/20 Hindsight

WHO AM I? HAVE YOU ASKED yourself this? Maybe more than once?

Even in my earliest memories, I reflected on life. The first I can recall occurred at 8-years-old. My elementary school was holding an election for the Student Council board. I was excited and day-dreamed about becoming the President of the Student Council.

And it was a dream.

I was not the most popular kid in school and I certainly wasn't the most confident. I lived in a beautiful yet small NH town where ethnicity segregation was replaced by economical segregation. You were either from the rich side of town or the poor side, and I was clearly not from the rich side of town. I was profoundly aware of this exclusion, even as a child, in the many things I could not have and how the differential of financial stature affected one's ability to gain social and peer acceptance.

Despite these obvious deterrents, my motivation to achieve my first little dream did not waver. I resolved to adopt a true democratic spirit and, following direction provided by my school principal and guidance counselor, I campaigned. I recruited a few of my closest friends to hand out flyers and flimsy mimeographed buttons during school recess. I forsook my recess period and the time for playing to greet the other students as they went to and from the school doorway to the playground.

On the day of the final voting count, I woke early and dressed as nicely as my wardrobe would allow. It had been many weeks of hard work and my confidence was tested. My mind filled with sinking thoughts of reality. Would my fellow candidates win over me?

They were more popular; in fact one girl was the prettiest in my class, one boy the most handsome and popular.

I recall thinking that morning as I rode the bus to school, *Why did I even enter the race? How could I have been so blind to their obvious advantages?*

Despite mounting insecurities, I went through the motions of the day. Each minute was scarier than the last, leading up to that final moment where, the votes counted, the winner was announced out loud on the intercom system for the entire school to hear.

Even now I remember where I was. I know in which room and at what desk I sat when the winners were read out loud. The hour leading up to that moment seemed like ten hours. As the Principal of our school read the results of each elected chair leading up to the President's position, I thought, I should have shot a little lower and run for a position of less stature! But it was too late. I was done for.

And then, my name was called,

"...this year's Student Council President will be Christine Stiles."

I had done it! All my sacrifices, hard work and efforts had paid off, and nobody was more surprised than me! The other candidates came from the various classes to concede and congratulate me, to shake my hand as I stood in amusement and disbelief. I had accomplished something far harder than even I realized until that moment.

I remember most profoundly the clear sense of pride I had that can only come from laying down extreme efforts towards achieving a dream or goal. I remember the sense of accomplishment and resounding faith that anything could be achieved with hard work and the drive that sets you apart from your competition.

Have you ever wanted something more than anyone else? And then got it? Then you understand. And if not, take note; because when you find yourself in a race in life for anything, you must want it badly enough to work for it harder than all others seeking the same goal you are fighting to achieve.

I can't explain how this small blip on the radar of my life has defined me. That moment in my youth set me on a course of greater confidence for the rest of my life. That one moment gifted me a true sense of my ability to define my life through hard work and effort.

I learned how setting goals you want to achieve is about SEEING the end when you start.

I learned that life is about taking many little steps towards a goal, inch by inch.

I learned how setting higher goals than are logically achievable help you stretch, work harder, and challenge thyself to reach previously unfound heights.

Finally, and most importantly, I learned the power of the dream. I learned that listening to positive, driving, inner beliefs wins out over listening to haunting insecurities that can paralyze and deny the dream.

There have been, and continue to be, specific life-moments that molded me as a person and a leader. Every road to success is long and arduous and not for the faint of heart—and mine has been no different. My life has been riddled with personal triumph, emotional growth, and unending reward. If the lessons learned during this little childhood story were all that I need to accomplish greatness in my career, this book would end here! Obviously, my life is the progression of like stories and sought-after dreams, some of which do not have this happy ending. It is in the difficult moments in my life that I learned my greatest lessons.

Why Title This Book Wise Eyes?

It has been 40 years since I ran for the Student Council President of my elementary school.

Once, years ago, I was asked, *What defined you as a child to seek out success?*

It was then that I realized how incredibly and profoundly ignorant I had been about my inequities compared to the advantages my competitors held. I understood how, in this story, my spirit and belief carried me through to victory.

Did my success come from strategy or acknowledgement of the obvious hurdles? No. Had I approached my goal of being President by accepting that I did not possess the financial means to buy expensive campaign buttons, to buy my constituents, to grease the palms of my peers, or draw on a large pool of established and existing friends, I would have never entered the race at all.

By dissecting the behavior that led me to that first leadership success, I came to understand that the same strengths and beliefs led me to great career success. Moreover, I still apply these methods and lessons to reach new heights.

My journey of self-reflection became one of discovery. I stumbled upon a course that consistently rewards me, both financially and spiritually. Most amazing about this epiphany was my understanding of how these lessons unswervingly keep me in an evolution of self-improvement and self-change.

As a successful leader and manager, I can honestly say one's ability to overcome all odds, to stay positive, to use your own weapons and diminish self-doubt is the most valuable strength one can possess. Fear and self-doubt are the greatest and most defiant enemies of all dreams.

It is not always possible to reach people who are inherently pessimistic and insecure. These people migrate to the negative, focus on the problems, and point out their challenges as hurdles they are unable to overcome. All of my coaching and all of my experience will not prevail; even my genuine guidance and repetitive preaching fails with people who cannot look in the mirror and make that initial and vital change to embrace self-awareness.

To open the doors to success, I believe a person must turn inward and acknowledge that they innately migrate to the negative and thus prevent themselves from achieving self-improvement. The title of this book, *Wise Eyes: See Your Way to Success!* shows the way. It begins with self-discovery.

The lessons in this book are illustrated by a series of stories and experiences that helped me, in an ever-evolving world, to overcome my inner doubts, steer the course, and ultimately achieve unfathomable success against seemingly incomprehensible odds. Be warned, these lessons only effect change if you will ask and answer the one and most vital question,

"Who am I?"

"You Can't Have A Million Dollar Dream with A Minimum Wage Work Ethic."

~Stephen C. Hogan

CHAPTER TWO

The Man in the Mirror!

A LESSON IN SELF ASSESSMENT

IT IS SAID THAT ONE CANNOT SEE the forest for the trees when standing in the forest. Thus, there is a need to take one out of their element and into a world that can open eyes, even eyes most closed to success.

Age is irrelevant in this. It does not matter how young or old you are when you take this valuable, first step toward achieving your success.

Income is irrelevant. It doesn't matter your means or your ample assets. Success is not disparate for those who are privileged. Success is not inherently prejudiced against any set of minorities, or whether you are from a particular ethnicity, financial prowess, sexual preference, or religious affiliation. Success is bestowed upon those individuals who can start from a place of genuine and honest self-acknowledgement.

My greatest personal growth has come from hearing the most painful words. I struggle with being sensitive to criticism, even when accurate and necessary. Instantly, my reaction is a knee jerk defense, to lash out. I have learned to curb this reaction, to instead sit back, let the message absorb, and think on it. This allows me to realize I need to make the suggested changes, or else provides me with insight into how to counter the critique with an appropriate response.

This is truly learned behavior and in hindsight, I admire those leaders who coached me, learning in the process that I am trainable, even though I am a wild horse bucking, hard to ride or hold onto. With time and persistence, I am coachable and can be lead by a harness down a path, but usually only after I show how high I can kick.

I am a fierce adversary if you decide to make me one. I will rise up if cornered, still to this day, I have fight in me to persevere; probably have pointed my gun at a few people wrongfully.

Conversely, I have found as a leader it is equally hard to deliver what I know will be painful criticism. Delivering difficult coaching and news is the double-edged blade that comes with personal growth. I have found the right way to say things. That has become easier for me over time because I see it for what it is worth—it is true self development.

And here is the value: once you discover who you are and are willing to face that person and start your journey from a place of understanding, you will recognize the truth I've found. The very best coach you can acquire is the guy who will work you to the bone, make you create better habits, be a mental physical trainer, and not be afraid to say to you the true things that need to be heard. That is the coach I strive to be.

I teach a vast array of professionals in and out of my specific field. These courses draw from my own success stories, those of great mentors and idols, and also from the pain and suffering of great losses and failure. I teach by sharing examples and stories that expose my innermost vulnerability, and even my greatest failures. By presenting my genuine self, I connect with people who cannot set a course for success through teachings that are pompous and self-serving, or conceited and condescending. I truly believe my teaching is effective because of my ability to admit my flaws and relate to my students through their insecurities and obstacles. I teach from a real place rather than to pretend I possess some incredible and untrue power that many teachers seem to tout once they have achieved success.

I start almost every class as I opened this book, asking you to ask yourself, "Who Am I?"

I teach with this same phrase, despite the specific lesson being taught. Stories teach a lesson and enable the student to open their eyes and to view the lesson, the circumstance, through a different lens. And the first story to embrace is your own.

Who Are You?

It is my hope that you will use this book to explore your own self-discovery process and begin your journey to achieve your dreams and goals. Here is an example of my opening exercise. I encourage you to pause here in your reading and complete the exercise.

Ask yourself the following questions and answer them with brutal honesty. Circle the number of your most common response to each question:

When I am asked to change, my reaction is:

1) I can't make this change.

2) Why do we need to make this change (and then be willing to try)?

3) This makes sense. I am glad it is changing.

When I speak with my peers at work, I am most likely to:

1) Agree with the complaints and join the commiseration

2) Listen and not participate with the gossiping

3) Be the voice of reason

When I am alone at home and starting a project or personal goal:

1) I have trouble getting started

2) I start but hardly ever finish

3) I finish all the projects I start

What do your Answers Mean?

What can be seen in the answers to the above three questions is your inherent thought process. I call these three the *Lion*, the *Tiger*, and the *Bear*.

Please review your answers and put yourself squarely into one of the three categories, the one which you believe is your most comfortable fit.

You are going to be a mix of the three but there are clear definitions and trends to your thought processes that place you more strongly in one over the others.

This exercise is not a science; rather a guide and you will gain the most by overlooking the overlap between categories.

The Lion

If you answered with all ones (1), you are a Lion. You are someone with great pessimism and disbelief in reaching goals. Maybe you have tried to reach goals on projects before this only to fail. Maybe you have not approached those goals with a plan or belief in the result of the goal. Maybe you can't see the end goal because you can't get past the first step. If you are in this category, much self-change is needed to set a course for success. How you make those changes will become an exercise in motivation to make this significant change in your life. It starts with picking a project, no matter how small or great. You will use basic planning techniques that teach how to get started and then take each step towards your goal.

It is a re-thinking process. When your natural mind does not provide business plans for any goal, then re-tooling of that thought process is necessary. Until you apply the key steps to project planning and achieve some form of success, you will continue down a path of self-doubt and disbelief. It is vital you start a project consciously aware of the profound change you are making for the rest of your life. You must be mindful that, by setting out on a path to achieve a true success story, you re-define who you are, and change your approach towards future projects and the inner belief that you have the ability to succeed.

The Tiger

If you answered with all twos (2) you are a Tiger. You are someone with the desire to succeed but a moderate level of innate self-doubt. Unlike a Lion in this lesson, you have the human characteristics of someone fighting internally between the belief that you can do it and the doubt that you can't do it. That battle will be won by first acknowledging you struggle with these two thought processes. Pull yourself over the fence of self-doubt by mapping out your projects and its many steps in a cyclical manner. Then take the first step, and then the next, and the next. You have the self-courage to do this already and the self-consciousness to push your mind to the more positive side simply by putting one foot in front of the other. Your win in achieving a project or plan will help you repeatedly apply these traits to future projects until your wins are coming more easily and more innately. Soon enough you will be someone who can set a course for success just by increasing your batting average.

The Bear

If you answered with all threes (3) you are a Bear. You are someone who keenly possesses the self-confidence and inner belief that you can and will achieve success at anything you set a course to achieve. So, the only hurdle you may have, if you haven't already achieved great success, is organization and planning. The great news here is you do not fight against a behavioral tide; you ride with the tide your mind has already gifted you. Where you decide to take your journey is merely an exercise in planning and execution. You are in a category of achievers and believers. This in and of itself, is a gift that you should not squander. Success is here for your taking, reach out and grab it.

Lions, and Tigers, and Bears...Oh My!

Now that you know whether you are a Lion, Tiger, or Bear allow me to entertain you a little with my own admissions.

First and foremost, you are not doomed if you are a Lion. In the initial part of my career I fell into a Lion state when facing most of my professional goals and hurdles. I struggled with a negative thought process and was not self-aware I was doing so.

For example, as a young professional, I took my first job in my field with no experience and immediately met an undying inner belief that I would not grasp the complexity of the tasks in my initial role. I would leave work every single night feeling defeated, frustrated and insecure. I awakened each day with a renewed belief in my ability to conquer challenges. As the day progressed, I was weighed down by an unrelenting fear of making no progress, and worse, that I might fail, which led to leaving at the end of the day once again feeling defeated.

It was not until I got angry with myself one evening and literally broke down emotionally that I found the strength to ignite the fight in me and conquer the obstacles, some of my own making, that faced me.

That night, from the depths of emotion, I saw what to do. I formed a plan! I would simplify the complexity of my job by compartmentalizing the components and master each task individually. This led me to accomplish each task and to total success.

What is the lesson here for you Lions? That discouragement is not all defeating. Lack of knowledge is a powerful deterrent, and it can bring you to your knees, but it doesn't need to keep you there. To overcome personal negative self-doubt, you must break down the larger hurdle in front of you into bite size pieces and take the path, one step at a time, fundamentally bringing you back to the entire goal setting process of simplifying a dream, project or goal into many little steps.

And here is a secret that I will share, one I believe to be vital: I didn't outwardly share my fears. While I am asking you to admit to yourselves your inherent thought process, I would be hypocritical if I didn't admit that while I was suffering from professional paralysis, I handled my doubts internally, faked most of my confidence at that age, and sought out answers from my resources privately and subtly. I strongly believe that while we all gain admiration from our admissions of inequities, we also must play a strategic game professionally to balance our forward push for improvement without creating a lot of public doubt. Our ability to show strength in the face of adversity is more profound in achieving help and improvement than loudly articulating self-doubt and failure.

One more secret I'll share is perhaps more personal than vital. In the two decades I have advanced my career from one position to the next, I set a conscious course to master my current and particular role while simultaneously seeking career advancement. I had an unquenchable desire and thirst to achieve the next phase or role in my profession. It is only in recent years that I have finally found the most fulfilling satisfaction in all my accomplishments. My focus has changed from constant improvement and conquering the next great thing to satisfaction in where I am today, and a desire to share with others, to teach what I know. This in and of itself, has been life changing for me. I am now good with watching others go ahead of me and fanning the flames of their quests for success instead of my own.

"Take the first step in faith. You don't have to see the whole staircase, just take the first step."

~Martin Luther King

CHAPTER THREE

Make Your Move Already!

A LESSON IN TRUST

THROUGHOUT MY ENTIRE LIFE AND career, I have watched people standing on the sidelines, waiting for the right time or best moment to jump into the race. Quite frankly I have often seen them miss the opportunity altogether.

There are endless quotes available online to remind us of how hard taking action is. There are entire books devoted to stepping out. There are common phrases we all use, such as: Take the First Step and Get Started Now that are meant to remind us to take action. What I think is really being said is, Stop being stuck! In other words, *Make your move already!* What are you waiting for?

Successful people, when asked what they would do differently, tell you they would have taken that first step sooner. I'll ask again, what are you waiting for?

Fear

I have a theory about why people don't get started. It's about fear. Fear of failure. Fear of disappointment or disappointing. Fear of getting started. Fear of not finishing. Fear is disabling.

Somehow, I have been able to muster the courage to overcome fear. I recognize, having managed people for a very long time, that this is not always the case. I have given a lot of thought to understanding why my experience with fear is different, and more to the point, how I can use this to guide others past their fears.

My personality is innately that of a person who is impatient for results. Even as a child, I pushed myself harder for results. Taking the first step is easy for me, I think easier than most as I want always to get in the race; I have always been anxious to get in the race.

Is that the key that unlocks fear? I think so. If you find fear is blocking opportunity, get in touch with that part of you that wants it now! (Whatever 'it' is.) If you find yourself in fear of failing, I remind you that the ultimate failure is never getting in the race. You must want the experience more than you fear it.

I have trucked around a poster with me from job to job. I was given it a very long time ago, several jobs ago in fact. It is a powerful Michael Jordon quote that represents my philosophy.

Picture a sweaty and hard wrought Michael Jordan suited up with beads of sweat blistering on his forehead, and these words,

> *"I've missed more than 9000 shots in my career, I've lost almost 300 games, 26 times I was trusted the game winning shot and missed, I have failed over and over and over again in life, and that is why I succeed."*

When I saw this, I completely understood what drove him and also what drove me. If fear of failing is what is keeping you from getting in the race, please know that failure will happen. Don't fear what you can't avoid.

Instead, choose to find great excitement and satisfaction in simply getting into the race and lift your goals up from there. Make your plan about finishing the race. Worry about winning the race once your comfort level for being in the race is enough. Then, set your eyes on winning. Steps, little steps, one by one; this is how you build—taking the first step into a winning plan.

I know we also have fear around ridicule and embarrassing ourselves. The fears are endless. I have been laughed at, bullied, cheated and manipulated in my lifetime, from the time I was a young girl to this very day. Know these truths:

There will always be people in the race we fear are more formidable. We will always, as human beings, have fears.

There will always be bad guys out there trying to make themselves feel more important by beating on the guy next to them. Anyone with half a brain knows that a man's chastise is typically an exposure of his own insecurity. Funny as that is, the IQ of the person doing the chastising is often not high enough to know he is exposing weakness.

Get Over Yourself and Call Upon Your Core

For me, the fuel I got from those who told me I could not do it, or would not amount to X, Y or Z due to my early economic stature, was exactly what I needed to stand on my head and prove them wrong. When others may have seen the heights I had to overcome and said, it's useless, I did not fear. When many told me I was wasting my time, I persevered. In fact, the more people told me I could not do something, the greater I wanted to prove them wrong.

I realize not everyone has something to prove. The reason we choose to get out of bed in the morning, our motivation, is different for each of us. If proving your mettle is not important to you, then find what you value, what matters to you. Find the core reason you want success and let that drive you out of your seat.

What does freedom to drive to success mean to you? First, you truly have to avoid listening to people around you who are not going to fan the flames of your drive and your desire to become a person driving towards a goal. You must surround yourself with people who you believe have similar desires.

When I look back at the pain I felt as a child, I recognize that I had an inner desire to rise up and prove others around me wrong. Eighteen years is a long time to wake up every day feeling like you are less than the kids you go to school with on the basis of economic disparity.

What I can tell you is this. The same children who picked on me, who were spoiled, rich kids handed everything on silver platters, many of them have far less than I do today—in measurable ways. They are not all happy people; they are not all necessarily wealthy people any longer. Many couldn't carry on the legacy of the life style their parents bestowed upon them. Some found richness in a different way.

I spend little time contemplating this. I take solace in knowing that while I may have been seen once as sad and sorry, as less because I was poor, today I have proven that their judgement of me was misplaced and was only the momentarily defining characteristic from a child's perspective. Now we are grown. Now we have bloomed into what we always were but could not see through the eyes of children.

The challenges I faced back then became wins: I worked two part-time jobs and drove myself to get great grades to earn scholarship monies for college while they were handed their education. I saved to buy name brand clothes (which my folks could not afford) so I could fit in, they were shopping and dining out with their parents and being handed these luxuries. I find joy, comfort, and gratitude knowing that I grew up to build a world of reality and certain security.

What was my lesson here? We can't pick our start in life, we can only steer the direction we go from there. Our birthplace and birth parents are not selected by us. Our destiny is our own responsibility. We rise from wherever we start; we choose our path out of poverty or we submit to it. Conversely, rich kids who are born financially fortunate must learn to maintain that lifestyle or fall from it. Touché!

I found that my childhood was rich with love and lessons, morality, and spirit. Money didn't define the richness of my life then and it still doesn't now. It is a byproduct of my desire to make a legacy, a worthy life, to give back, and to experience what is out there. My success has been measured by overcoming odds, proving my ability to climb an invisible ladder, breaking new ground and achieving comfort in my life to provide security and safety for my son. A bonus to my success is having the opportunity to give back genuine life lessons and to teach and coach others to be the best they can be!

Our childhood does not define us. I knew even as a little girl that my childhood was just a step in the direction of my dreams. Nobody could convince me—even when I had every reason to believe I might never leave the trailer park—that I would be stuck in that place in life. I was too busy planning and making my next move!

My life has been a series of first steps over and over. Some of those steps were leaps forward and others proved to set me back but nonetheless, I have kept moving. Each step has been significant in its own measurable way. When I look back, my life has been like time stamped milestones, defining a path that I can easily trace from there to here.

I promise you, it's never too late to Make a Move! I am still building new dreams, making new plans, and overcoming new odds. The possibilities are quite endless! Just take the first step

"I will have the moral courage to make my actions consistent with my knowledge of right and wrong. Till I die I will not remove mine integrity from me."

~ Job 27:5

CHAPTER FOUR

Do All with Integrity

WHEN THE DUST SETTLES, IT IS AL-WAYS THE GOOD GUYS WHO ARE LEFT STANDING

IT IS PREFERABLE TO MAKE A MOVE on our own terms. There are times however when circumstances force change and when the only true control we have is how we choose to face and embrace the changed situation.

I took countless first steps. I made many moves from the teller line of a Massachusetts based credit union all the way to the helm of a national mortgage company, not once, but twice. They say lightning doesn't strike twice, and the same is true for breaking glass ceilings. It is hard to do over and over with the starting point each time being a new company; a new leadership to which you must prove to that you have the ability, experience, and wisdom to lead a sales force to great success because you have more inspiration and more literal banking experience in building superior financial success for organizations than anyone else. I have been fortunate to find progressive organizations that saw greatness in me and savvy thinking men who would place me either in the driver's seat or shot gun to the driver. In either position, I was allowed to navigate the company's national sales force.

Oddly enough, banking is not where I expected or planned to be. Throughout my entire youth, I sought a career in the health field; and even entered college with this in mind. Almost from my first job in a bank, I found myself in love with the fast-pace and competitive nature of the banking industry, in a field that provided almost two decades of growth before taking a sharp left turn that challenged my livelihood and professional existence.

There are times when, no matter how strong the vision we have, flexibility becomes the key to success. In 2007, one thing was for sure if you were a Loan Officer, you were either losing your current job, starting a new job, or repeating both over and over for the next couple years. While the mortgage industry as we knew it underwent a dramatic face lift, appendectomy, and repeated colonoscopy, what was left when it all shook out were a bunch of battle-scarred, true blue believers!

The real sales guys who believed their careers and flames would not be extinguished by an overzealous regulatory environment, an angry mob of consumers, and a fleeting and diminishing job market were somehow still standing, albeit staggering under a new load.

Due to the regulation and licensing changes, what emerged was a compliance minded mortgage originator who had to meet personal and arguably invasive and unfair standards. Requirements like personal credit and criminal background checks weeded out a lot of prior good mortgage sales guys. Yes, those mortgage originators who were left became the soldiers of this industry. What was never really spoken of was the integrity, grit, and perseverance of the survivors who were beat down by an entire world that had not predicted the perfect storm. I've had the pleasure of leading many of them through that storm.

I found myself at the helm of one company when the proverbial crap hit the fan. I learned what real leadership meant when faced with closing a company that I had spent over a decade building. I didn't know then though how rewarding it would be to lead so many originators to higher ground to become the first line of defense against an angry society of haters from all sides. I can't recall how many long conversations I had defending against mainstream media which had run all the victim stories. It would have helped to show that not all mortgage companies were corrupt, that not all mortgage originators were untruthful, and that many of us truly and sincerely had done our jobs as we were trained, guided, and regulated to perform. In truth, the best interest of the borrowers, for many of us, was always the number one priority. But I digress, this is water now under an old and fading bridge, thankfully.

Today, licensure requirements are more standardized, they serve to educate and protect the consumer. Loan Officer Commission is no longer based on the interest rate system, which protects the consumer. What is the most invigorating for me are the weathered soldiers. I see loan officers who had to hang up their refinance hats and completely redesign themselves and reemerge by learning the purchase business. These are the dedicated professionals in home financing who learned a new way to do business, who now do ten times the trust building to one eighth the customer pool, for a much longer life cycle.

I see companies that rebuilt their race cars while they were in motion on the race tracks and have done so successfully, like AnnieMac. I see loan officers who starved their way back to a better market, many who got here by the skins of their teeth and finally are reaping market reward. Yes, the sun is shining. Remembering how far we've come is a great reminder of how strong we all are, how good we are, how grateful we are, and how luck has had little to do with our survival. I am more compassionate to my competitor as my competition today is another soldier like me who survived. To that guy or gal, I owe the same debt of gratitude for helping us keep the boat afloat.

What is profound for me is that companies like mine get it right in their hiring. Today, the quality of the mortgage loan originator, both new and experienced, is a well-educated, licensed, and honest sales person who has informed choices about where they go to originate a loan. Companies like mine must be a polished suitor, worthy of their time and attention. It's a classier existence, it's a purer breed of sales people and I find it quite humbling and satisfying to see! There's no doubt that today's mortgage originator is someone who, without question, has the customer's best interest in mind.

Why? Because today the hoops that originators must pass through are not for the thin skinned. These professionals have worked hard to survive, they've helped rebuild the trust and the faith in an economy almost completely desecrated. They have one by one held up the weight of the industry's past sins and together, slowly but surely, emerged winners of their own personal career battles while winning wars with their companies.

Long gone are the sales guys who wanted to go to the fishing hole for an hour and fill up their two buckets. They are no doubt somewhere selling cars, furniture, and cell phones. The true-blue guys and gals who have consistently been honest are the originators who are still here, who made this a career, who always had their hearts in the right places, and who fought for (and won!) their seats at the table.

I look around this industry today with pride. I, too, have lived through the battle and emerged a stronger professional. When I ask myself, *"How did anyone survive what happened to this business?"* I know from having not fled from a single day of the horror that we persevered; that we absorbed the public criticism, the scarlet letter wearing days of the mortgage finance world. We stood, and we knew in our heart of hearts that many of us come to work every day wanting to do good by our customers.

Suffice it to say when countries like Norway and companies like Countrywide and Merrill Lynch fall victim to a *surprise* bubble that pops and leaves them trying to shrink in an impossible time frame; it truly is the Perfect Storm.

There is something to be said for the skeleton crew that weathers a storm together. Ultimately the fact that thousands of good loan officers stayed standing and weathered the incomparable changes including a massive pay cut, is impressive. The ultimate upside was that they became stronger and in the end, they owned more market share than when they started. Those types of moments, months and years in this case, will bond people in ways that movies and books will be written about for years to come.

I know in my darkest moments having lost my job at the helm of a Fortune 500 division of banking after a decade, to start over as a small manager of a market branch, was humbling. What was gratifying, and ultimately life changing, was to look at the war-torn carnage and realize what I saw in the eyes of guys and gals who were left was an appeal for direction and someone to lead.

My income was traded for the cause and that was true for every person left standing. People who probably wanted to flee, but this was all they knew and others who believed if they just hung in, that one day all would be good again. Now here we are...and it is good again.

It can be said that many people entered the mortgage field for income and wealth. Today I think it's true that the majority are here because the American dream of home ownership is still at the forefront of our world economy.

Integrity does prevail over greed and the desire for us to help each other as human beings is more profound than anything else in life.

"You have the business you earned."

~ Matthew Rowan

CHAPTER FIVE

Make a New Plan, Stan!

IT TAKES A SYSTEM

SOMEWHERE IN MY ADVOCACY FOR success, and when I was a young age, I began to realize the power of planning. Early on I did my planning with merely a pencil and paper and I had no real format. Nonetheless, what I did have was a written plan to follow.

During my early professional life, I was put in a business planning class and began to learn the structure around planning: the vision, the tasks, and the execution.

Then I attended a life changing leadership summit in New York City. The guest list was limited, the invite was elite, and the leadership line up impressive: Rudy Giuliani, Richard Branson, Jack Welch, Colin Powell, Ann Jung, and one of the many Yahoo CEOs.

The topic of discussion was open, and I sat with pen in hand, wide eyed and appreciative to be one of the guests. I held a national position within my company at that time and the discussion on business tactics was both relevant and provided empowering food for my creative mill.

Are you a note taker? Taking the notes is a huge part of my learning style, and I discovered early on that I have an ability to create organization out of chaos, even as I take notes. This gift rang true during this amazing leadership summit. I realized as I wrote down the words of importance from each leader that a clear and concise pattern of planning steps rang through. When it was all reviewed later in the quietness of my home, I saw commonalities amongst the speakers that revealed a core truth: all plans have eight philosophies at their core.

Those eight philosophies were represented in the habits and beliefs of all the leaders in that room in New York City. These eight principles truly are the unwritten plan of success. And these same eight philosophies can be adopted and followed to accomplish all things you intend on doing!

I have embraced the original eight concepts and put my own spin on them to create my own process, which I teach to this day, and have documented in a short film that can be found on my website.

Following these eight philosophies, anyone can write a plan, execute on the steps in the plan, and discover that it works. These eight philosophies have guided me through massive change, consolidations, mergers, and acquisitions. Holding true to these philosophies has enabled me to work in a male domi-nated field and rise to the top despite my gender. I have broken glass ceilings at Fortune 500 companies and have done so simp-ly because I put my head down, hatched my plan, and then exe-cuted on its many steps, one by one.

Using these philosophies, I continue to take sales teams from last to first place and help others map a path to their goals and dreams.

In the next eight chapters, I share this exclusive eight-step process using real life stories and examples of both success and failure. I have proven this to myself, and to my students, over and over again. And you can do the same.

I am excited to share with you my eight core philosophies. They are generic enough to be applied to a business plan for any field, so I hope you will put this to good use!

CHAPTER SIX

Eight Core Philosophies for Success in Business Planning

Core Philosophy: Plan Your FUTURE

THE FUTURE

MY BELOVED BOSTON WAS BOMBED on April 15, 2013 during one of its historical marathons. As part of the grotesque gravity of one of our country's first memorable tragedies of that magnitude, Boston experienced the complete lock down of several counties for 48 hours while a man hunt was conducted.

Four million people remained locked in their homes. Boylston street's normal hustle was reduced to a barren, desolate urban desert, as was every street in a 60-mile radius. Meanwhile, an unprecedented man hunt ensued to the point of fruition over the final 48 hours of this nightmare tragedy.

After weeks and months of survival and recovery, dozens of heart wrenching physical comeback stories culminated in former victims running the marathon a year later, less one or two limbs.

Courage? Yes.

Fight? Yes.

Heart? Yes.

Will. I am describing a will that is driven by an emotional desire to succeed; a will that overcomes physical hurdles to deliver a resurgence of the body through the pushing of the mind. I could tell you endless stories of the power a mind has over a body. And it amazes me how few people will battle their own minds or recognize when their minds are steering them wrong. Will is key to everything in life, and it drives you to your goal.

Age is irrelevant in this. It does not matter how young or old you are when you take this valuable, first step toward achieving your success.

Planning for your future requires a vision of the end goal as it fits into a plan. We all want a bright future; that's human nature. Let's take this basic desire a step further than hope for a rosy tomorrow:

How will you ensure that future?

In what facet of your life do you have plans and take action?

Are you thinking about personal health? Wealth? A hobby? A milestone?

Everything you plan for must have a finish line. And it does not end there. Even after you plan, execute, and achieve, there is continued maintenance to remain within the landscape of your goal. Say you want to get a new job or earn a greater amount of income. When you get the new job and salary, the goal morphs into a plan for maintenance—you want to keep the job. And yet, without visualizing the finish line at the very beginning, your maintenance plan is useless because the goal will remain unfulfilled.

In 2003 I received a hard-fought promotion to District Manager of the Boston area district center made up of approximately 125 people. Eighty-eight of those employees were sales people and their managers, the rest were operations folk.

The district was in last place. The fact that Boston was in last place and complaints had risen about the seated manager bode well for me getting a glass ceiling shot.

I had been trying to reach the ranks of District Manager for two years. When I took on the job, I also had the mentorship of two key leaders holding decision-making seats in the company: my then regional manager and my current CPO. Both saw in me grit and experience enough that they made the choice to help me to be the first woman to hold a seat, at this level, in the history of the company.

When I dug in, I had just finished a one-year long leadership program with my then company that could not have been timelier. The program taught me the skills in practical and practiced application on all things senior leaders needed to hone.

The leadership program was amazing. I learned analytics, speaking, conflict management, growth, forecasting, training, and motivation. And of course, I took all of this on while working my normal job and flying all around the country for these leadership meetings. On top of that we were put on teams with people we didn't know which in and of itself required professionalism and patience.

At the start, the CEO said we would get training by fire, equivalent to a bachelor's degree in business management, and at the end, WE would build the company's next five-year plan.

When I was set free to be with my new team and my promotion, which came right at the end of this year, I had everything I needed to build upon. In fact, I just mimicked what I had learned.

I started with assessing, and I interviewed every single employee. I knew that I could not build a strong foundation or following if I didn't understand first what was broken (or perceived to be broken). Furthermore, I needed to bond with them in a way that made them feel heard and protected.

We called our plan *Movin' on Up*, and we wore pins every day as a reminder of being in last place and how the work done by each of us would make a difference.

You can see that outcome now on my video section of my website, under the title of *Movin' On Up*. It is now one of the crowning moments of my career because we moved mountains and we fought our way, not only out of last place, but all the way to the top. Once we had momentum, no one could catch us.

We had been counted out and laughed at many times. As the only female manager that was hard to take. At times, I felt inwardly insecure. As I saw our plan in action, I quickly realized we were going to be a contender for the top draw.

And yet, I did not smack talk, I did not boast. I knew I would have my moment. I sat through bragging by others who won previously at District manager meetings.

One consistent winner, who was arguably overconfident said, "I use this trip as my annual family vacation."

Of course, we all laughed. The other managers looked at me as if to say, *Honey, you have no clue.*

And me? I bided my time, telling them in my mind, *Just wait.*

I played a strategic game and busted my butt, worked my tail off, while not acting like I necessarily was. I worked when other teams rested.

I also had done my homework. I knew that Boston had the second average highest loan balance, and of the 14 other districts I was competing against, we had a great chance to pick up speed quickly. Based on how the points were weighted (units verses volume), volume was in our favor.

People think I have a big mouth because I like to talk; but they do not realize I will die with a thousand secrets if keeping those secrets is the key to getting ahead. I am not stupid and that is where some under-estimated me. That same manager bragging about family vacations had to hand me my first-place trophy in Switzerland. Every underdog gets their day, they say!

I have had people share with me seriously insane goals, which I may have raised a private eyebrow to, and then I've watched them achieve the seemingly impossible. And I've seen people fail, succumbing to my speculation their goal was too high. I really believe setting goals is about your personal will. And it does not hurt to have the tools and training to succeed in imposing your will on reality.

Muhammad Ali wrote,

> "Champions aren't made in gyms. Champions are made from something they have deep inside them—a desire, a dream, a vision. They must have the skill and the will. But the will must be stronger than the skill."

I had his image on a poster with this quote hanging in my office for many years. I am certain many of my employees dismissed me for being corny because I quoted this. And yet, this quote resonates with me. I feel it. I have written my own personal philosophy around emotion and will and all the things that emotionally drive us. I figured out long ago, I am capable of just about anything I put my mind to. I have come from unimaginable lows to reach unfathomable heights with nothing more than my will.

The Blueprint

Planning all things starts with the vision of the finish line. Your future state is the end game.

At this time, pause in your reading, and let's create your blueprint. On a piece of paper, write the number 1 and the words Blueprint for Business Planning next to it. Then add the words Future and Vision next to that.

Now write down the number that represents your annual earning in that future end state. In this example, let's say your current income is $100,000 and your goal is to increase it. You would write your blueprint like this:

1. My Blueprint for Business Planning—Future and Vision: earn $200,000 annually.

This is the beginning of your blueprint. We will fill in additional lines as we explore all eight of these core philosophies.

CHAPTER SEVEN

Eight Core Philosophies for Success in Business Planning

Core Philosophy: Your CURRENT State

ASSESS YOUR STARTING POINT

IN ORDER TO UNDERSTAND and maintain a clear vision of where you are going, you need to know where you currently are and measure the distance between the reality and the vision. I have created a formula for gauging that distance. You will apply this formula to your real goal, of course. However, to understand the process, we will use the goal of an increase in annual income written on your example blueprint.

1. Current State (Reality)

Use the annual income that you are currently earning. (If this is a real goal, you will want to be aware that if this is a salary, that number is simple to assess. If you are self-employed, then you need to actuate your run rate into an annualized number or use a 12-month historical average.)

2. Future State (Clear vision, Statement of the Goal)

Now compare the two numbers, your Future earnings goal with your Current earnings.

3.   Gap

What is the gap? Write it on your blueprint.

Creation of your entire plan and development of the other six philosophies to achieve your goal, your vision of your future state, is based on your ability to maneuver yourself between your current state and a future state and then maintain.

This formula works as well with a goal that is not financial. Another example might be weight loss plan.

- Current State: Weight is X

- Future State: Weight is Y

- Gap: 20 Pounds lighter

Your future state has you weighing Y. You currently weigh X and the gap is 20 lbs. Now you know the distance between the two states. You then see yourself weighing Y in the future state with an expectation that once there, you will maintain.

The formula is deliberately simplistic, and the theory is easily applied to all things you want to plan for. And yet....

Are your goals and plans simple? Rarely. Specific yes, and in most instances, also complex. There are key philosophies around goal setting and planning we now need to address before we can fill in the blanks and additional steps of your Blueprint for Business Planning. For example:

- Is your goal too lofty?

- Is your goal too easy?

- Are you willing to stretch outside your comfort zone? How far?

- Is this a serious, life-improving change?

- When you hold up your plan at a later date, will you claim victory or see forsaken results?

Self-Assessment

Have you ever seen a dog chase a car? I am sure you have! Have you ever wondered how far that dog is willing to run to catch the car? Well, the answer is whether the dog believes it can catch the car. If the car remains at a tangible distance to the dog chasing it, you will probably see that dog run for miles before either tiring in the chase or eventually catching the car. Conversely, if the car pulls ahead a measurable distance and creates a gap, the dog will stop trying when it realizes the car has driven out of reasonable sight. Goal setting follows the same philosophy.

If your future state and vision is a long distance from your current state, to sustain the energy to achieve it, you must take a series of steps that are measured out and that keep the goal you're currently working to achieve within a reach you can clearly envision. Plans are successful not because people sprint at the finish line, rather because they see each step; take the first, then the next, the next, and the next.

This is especially true when your plan requires a long measure of time to achieve. Sustain and feed your vision, each step along the way. Continuously moving towards your goals is an exercise in keeping the car far enough in front of you to keep you running, but not too far that you give up.

I have a saying, *Do not set your goals so high you need binoculars to see them.* This comes first when I teach goal setting.

Next, we'll look at the science behind the power of planning using a few known college studies.

CHAPTER EIGHT

Eight Core Philosophies for Success in Business Planning

Core Philosophy: Key Stakeholders

ANCHOR

ANCHOR YOUR PLAN! There is a philosophy in planning called anchoring. This is where you make it be known to key people in your life that you are venturing into a new plan.

These are pivotal people in your life who help you achieve your personal and professional goals. Of course, the key stakeholders for each plan is likely to be different, but the overall group tends to be the same people for most plans: Your spouse / partner / boyfriend / girlfriend, your boss / manager, and a peer or partner in the plan.

For example, if you were to quit smoking or start a new diet, you would let everyone in your immediate sphere of influence know about this quest. If you plan to succeed you want their support. You make it public because it keeps you on track knowing others are watching.

Conversely, if you didn't want an audience, you would keep that plan quiet. You would tell no one and then, if you failed, only you would know.

While I appreciate privacy as much as the next gal or guy, I also know that keeping it to yourself is an emergency exit for a plan and a recipe for failure in planning. You MUST anchor your plan, make it as public as possible, and be willing to live up to that audience—regardless of the result.

In the college studies I examined (and from which I teach) students voluntarily capsulated their future incomes at graduation time, twenty years forward. When measured, those who voluntarily wrote down where they would be in 20 years represented 80% of the overall wealth of the entire graduating class when they represented only a 5% participation group. What does that tell us? It tells us, when your plan is anchored, public, and measured, you will work harder to achieve success. In many ways it's a simple way to trick yourself into compliance.

Once you have all eight philosophies written in your blueprint, share the plan with your key stakeholders and make your plan as public as you feel comfortable. For example, post it on social media, send out an email, speak about it within interested or vested groups. How public, how deep you go is your choice. It is absolutely necessary to at least tell your key stakeholders.

CHAPTER NINE

Eight Core Philosophies for Success in Business Planning

Core Philosophy: Daily Action Steps

ACTION

THE DAILY ACTIONS AND STEPS it takes to achieve your overall plan provide a core to get you from Point A to Point B. To build your plan, you will first look at the gap analysis we wrote out on your blueprint (philosophy one and two).

What was the distance between your future desired outcome and your current state? Let's use weight loss here as an example. Say you are currently 170 pounds and you would like to weigh 130 pounds. The difference is 40 pounds.

Consider your timeline now and set incremental milestones. You have done your research and discovered that the best results for maintaining and keeping weight off happen when the pounds come off slowly and methodically. You decide to spend the next year losing this weight.

Gap divided by timeline duration = milestones (40/12=3.333)

To identify your milestones, divide your weight loss across 12 months. This shows that you must lose a little over 3 pounds per month. This is the formula you will use to measure your monthly incremental steps towards your future state.

Now you need to break down your plan's timeline and milestones into the daily tasks and your new plan of action to achieve this goal. For example:

- You're not currently exercising so you will promise to do a series of some resistance exercise three times a week for a period of 20 minutes.

- This workout regime represents month one and two and you will re-examine, change, and add onto the workout routine every 60 days.

- You will cut out fattening foods you currently eat.

- You will make a list of foods that are now prohibited.

- You will throw out foods in your cupboards that contain a lot of sugar and preservatives.

- You will eat smaller more frequent meals.

- You will shop more carefully.

This example clearly shows that you are outlining and recognizing the changes that must be made to your daily habits for you to make a fundamental shift in both mindset and activities to start marching towards your goal.

This technique and philosophy is applicable to all things. Let's look at another example and apply it to sales or income goal setting.

Starting from where you are to where you want to be you calculate a difference of 100K in income. Meaning your new future state has you earning an annualized income of 100k more than current. You divide that by 12 months and you arrive at a difference of 8,333.00 per month in additional income that you need to generate to achieve this goal. This is your gap analysis.

Current State = $100,000. Future State = $200,000. Gap = $100,000. Annualize and divide across 12 months (100,000/12=8,333).

Now let's apply some analytics to this. You currently sell mortgages. Your average commission on each is approximately 2,000. You have been closing two units per month, and when you divide your YTD income into how many mortgages you have closed, to hit your goal you need to more than double your production.

This is where that philosophy in goal setting was put to the test in the very first step of planning; when you compared your goal to being a stretch verses too far to reach or easily obtainable. You will have to decide now if that is achievable. If you believe it is, the next part of your daily task planning will have to involve the ability to market, spend time selling, and increase your rate of return on your efforts by more than 100%.

The only question remaining is, can I do this and what will it take to do it? In this example, maybe the goal is too high. Maybe you back that down to 75K increase and lower the added needed sales per month to 2 units, making it far more reasonable, but not easy, to reach. The value in using this formula is to precisely see each incremental step you must achieve and clearly visualize the gap you must bridge within your daily timeline to achieve the future state!

Who's Your Boss?

Are you self-employed? Did you choose to become your own boss for the flexibility of your schedule? Yes? Raise your hand as you sit there at home alone. You know who you are! I am sure that each of you who made this choice quickly found that to build a business takes a tireless, self-starting and finishing work ethic. It takes significantly more effort during the first few years to launch. Assuming you've done an excellent job in planning and growing your business, in a few years you can get into some sort of groove, although the tireless self-starting and finishing work ethic never gets dropped. In business planning, whether managing yourself, a person, or group of people, to increase business the process is the same. You must take the time to create your blueprint, follow through with each of these steps outlined in these philosophies, and even outline your five days a week into a schedule of start and finish, prospecting and analysis, marketing and appointments. You must know your daily tasks are leading to your finish line in your plan, measurably. (We will talk about measuring your business plan as one of our final steps.)

As a rule of thumb, you want to stay in the selling pocket for four out of five days, a minimum of 50% of an 8-hour day or for four hours for four days. 4x4 we call this!

What Inspires You?

There is an endless supply of powerful quotes from a bevy of hugely successful people, celebrities, sports figures, and the like.

I have my own favorites, many of which you will see throughout this book. The last step in your Core Philosophy is to fill in your own quote. It can be your own words. It may be a quote from someone you admire. Perhaps it's a quote from someone anonymous or an amalgamation of several quotes from multiple sources.

Whatever you choose, own it. It must represent how you feel about the plan you have in place for whatever improvement, whatever change you are making to your future state. Once you find it, write it boldly into your Blueprint for Business Planning!

Keep in mind, people business-plan vacations, they business-plan retirement, they may business-plan a wedding or a make-over or a plan to quit a bad habit. People by nature want to do well, and we find our motivation in peaks and valleys. This is true for all of us.

I am not sure when I became self-aware in my job as a sales person that when I was in the saddle, or hot, that I would stay there. Instead of doing four hours of sales like I planned, when I was hot, I would keep going and sell all day. In one hot day I might accomplish the equivalent of three days of sales.

The same is true with your quest for achieving new things in planning, whatever it is. You are going to have good days and bad days. Remember, a plan doesn't need to be thrown out the window because you had a bad day. I always say, don't quit your diet because you ate a Twinkie! Seriously! Every day is a new day. We have this great gift of renewal every single day, and when forming new habits, it takes time to disengage the auto pilot your brain is on.

What Inspires Me

Emotion is the driving force behind all human intellect, accomplishment, and success. If you cannot feel where you are going, you cannot SEE it either. My life's goals and accomplishments both personally and professionally have all come from one place, my deep inner emotion.

In fact, the success I have had in sales, business management, and life has come from my ability to express and share my emotion, evoke emotion while teaching, and finally, through helping others express their own emotions, I have unleashed their inner drive and motivation to succeed. Harvesting your emotion allows you to experience the spirit and soul of success.

In life we have all faced and will face again many obstacles and adversity. Our success in recognizing these obstacles and overcoming them lies in our ability to seek knowledge and apply it. Anyone can read a book. Anyone can take a class. Really successful people are driven to run towards that goal and achieve that success because they are emotionally motivated to do so. Thus, they learn and apply that knowledge much faster and far more easily.

This is my Core Philosophy. This, in some form, is a part of every blueprint I create for myself. Take the time, I implore you, to find your core, and embrace it across everything you do.

CHAPTER TEN

Eight Core Philosophies for Success in Business Planning

Core Philosophy: Enhancers and Support

WORK ENVIRONMENT ENHANCERS

YOUR CORE PHILOSOPHY, once identified, will grow and change as you do, and yet always remains at heart the same. The reason this is true is really a basic one, and also one that many people overlook.

Your working environment has to be conducive to proper focus, provide for convenient on-hand tools and systems, and be free of distraction. Make it a place where you can sit in the pilot seat and fly the plane without interruption, from your morning starting point to your destination at the end of day. It needs to be reflective of your personality, warm, and comfortable.

It also needs to be organized and well kept. We have all seen that cubicle or office where you enter, and you wonder how the individual is operating at all based on the condition of their working environment. Never mind the projected image to potential clients and the damage that may be done to future business; consider the perception of your subordinates, peers, and managers. What we do projects an image of control or chaos.

You are either out in front of the parade marching like a queen and king, or you are getting run over by the parade.

This is a quote I use often, and one I came up with when teaching organizational skills years ago. It is so true. Every day I think of whether I am marching out in front or getting run over. My advice to you is to stay in front of the parade as much as you can. That's winning to me. Not perfection, just percentages of winning.

I advise my students to pick a time of year to clean-slate your work environment; to start over. I happen to like January 1st for this. Seems like a good time to start anew. I usually will take everything off my desk until it's bare, including emptying out the drawers. I will clean and polish the desk. I will set new desk calendars on it, freshen supplies, buy some new trinkets, and certainly set it up where all my greatest tools are within arm's length. I will take down all business cards, sticky notes and such. I will reorganize and start with a bare pin board in front of me. I will hand write Dos and Don'ts for that year. Personal ones, like *I will not eat bread,* or *I will work out 5X a week.* I leave my professional goals to my blueprint for business plans.

Health and Well-Being Enhancers

Enhancers do also come in the form of your health, your mental well-being, and your living environment. To clearly work proficiently, creatively, and securely you must be in a healthy environment. For many years I worked until 1 or 2 am. I didn't exercise and ate poorly. In the morning I dragged myself out of bed, propped myself up with two cups of strong coffee and ran that fuel line to its bitter end, then re-fueled with more coffee in the afternoon.

That was my cycle. Sure, I had moments of brilliance. The process worked, to a degree. Yet I was missing and overlooking a critical element. The true growth of my mind, my sustainable efforts, and my highest results came when I adopted a healthy life style and added this commitment to my core philosophy.

This choice is yours. If your life resembles my old one, I strongly advise a change. When you decide to move to the healthier end of the scale and change even three things about your life in a given year, you will thank me.

In the past two years I chose to stop drinking iced coffee and soda. They were both filled with calories and they had empty sugars that helped raise and drop my energy levels. Not great for going on auto pilot at work. I also cut out sweets and bread. I implemented a 3-times a week work-out routine two years ago that I now do 5-times a week. When I started, I could barely stand the elliptical for five to ten minutes. I could do maybe a dozen sit-ups and 10 pushups. Today I do 30-45 minutes of cardio, 200 sit-ups, and 60 pushups almost daily. I am strong of body and mind.

I taught myself how to eat healthy, and I do not see it as a diet. I see it as a way of living. I once hated salad and I now crave it. Due to these changes, I have a higher stress threshold, I have a longer sustainable energy level that does not peak and wane, and I am far more mentally balanced. My stress is left at the gym or with the sweat on my towel. I highly recommend this to anyone. As a result, I am also 40 pounds lighter and in the top shape of my life with visible results as I near my fiftieth birthday.

What enhancers will you add to your core philosophy and include in your blueprint and incorporate into your daily life?

CHAPTER 11

Eight Core Philosophies for Success in Business Planning

Core Philosophy: Obstacles and Hurdles

ADVERSITY

HAVE YOU EVER FAILED at a business plan, goal, or path? In hindsight, what would you say about that experience? Would you see the clear mistakes that threw you off? Was there an all-in-one destroyer of your plan?

So many times, when we have a bad day it trickles into our week. So many times, when we have a bad week it becomes our bad month, our bad year. Adversity is hard to overcome, especially when unexpected. And yet....

Would you stop your diet all together if you ate a half gallon of ice cream today? Or would you wake tomorrow and start over again, determined to have more will power today?

How many wrong steps does it take to fall out of new, more productive habits and back into the old, less productive ones?

I have been on a three-year personal exercise plan. Midway through, due to unexpected circumstances that mainly had to do with travel, I broke my cycle of exercise and allowed the break to almost completely derail me. Almost. I picked myself up, adjusted the plan, and renewed my commitment. I regained my strength built back up to the level of daily exercise I enjoy today. Accept that obstacles will show up. In every plan, it's important to expect the unexpected and to prepare. Why do you carry a spare tire in the trunk of your car? Because a flat tire can happen in any journey and the spare will get you to the repair shop to assess and continue moving forward. Bolster your plan; cement the steps you take by considering in advance what could cause the tire to go flat and how you will progress despite it.

Obstacles and Hurdles

First, you must think of all the obstacles that could derail your specific plan. What are they? Time? Money? Resources? Be specific when you write these down.

What are your hurdles? What are the things that might slow you down but not knock you out of the game? Kids schedules? Bad market? Think of past adversity that derailed plans and of future and current challenges.

The Remedies

Once you write these down, apply a remedy to each. If you said *time* then write how you can overcome it, get more time towards your plan. Write a schedule if need be. Dissect your existing work hours. What are you doing with your time now?

Once you have these obstacles and hurdles laid out, you can apply your remedies and be more prepared as they present themselves.

There are a couple of golden rules to be sure you include, so remember:

1. Be prepared with a plan to overcome the obstacles and hurdles that will occur!

2. Everyone has real life factual reasons to sway from a plan. Life happens, takes us off our game. How quickly we get back in is up to us. Look in the mirror and be honest with your own self. Don't make excuses!

3. Start fresh every day! Every day is a new opportunity! Don't throw the plan out if you fall off the wagon today! Fact. You will have bad days. Don't allow those to be weeks and then months.

Here is a powerful story I'd like to share that illustrates this philosophy. except for myself, all participants in this story must remain anonymous.

At this particular time in my career a lot of things were going right. I was in a great place and successfully managing a branch and rather large team. One day an underwhelming employee, who had promised in his hiring far greater production than he was delivering, walked into my branch with two peers he had convinced to resign. It was quite the scene.

In a series of unfortunate events that followed, I was relieved of my duties. Now, that is the cliff note version of a dramatic series of events that I would rather not relive. At the end of the day if the team is falling apart, no matter how strong the other members are, the coach is always the one who is let go.

In this instance, the repercussions for me were even worse— I was asked to stay on in a different capacity. This was easily the lowest moment in my career and it felt as though wrong had been done to me, by several parties, but especially by my immediate boss. I am still not certain, to this day, whether this boss was selfishly motivated to make this unfortunate move.

In the end, after going home and assessing what had happened and what lead led up to the final actions, I decided that I would not run from the situation. Instead, I would take the new job I was given, and I would put my head down, and work hard at it. Mind you, the manager who succeeded me, in a rather cruel move on the bosses' part, had been my live-in boyfriend who worked at the same company.

That made for rather difficult home life for a while; but he was one of the people who convinced me to rise above it and in true fashion of his class, he helped me through an otherwise devastating time by defending me, standing by me, and allowing me the time and space to recover and heal.

How difficult was this obstacle for me to overcome? What kind of mental shifts do you think I had to make to get past this hurdle? The fortitude that it took for me to recover was unprecedented in my experience and it actually took a couple of years to correct my path. What it took was sheer mental strength, acceptance of the situation, forgiveness to those who had done me wrong, humility to accept a lower position, and renewal of my faith to commit to another job and prevail.

In hindsight, that horrendous day led to one of the greatest learning experiences of my life. I was set upon a different career path in a new role that brought me all the way to where I am today. Experiencing the lowest of the low showed me more about my own self than I ever thought possible and probably provided a few on-lookers incredible front row seats to a comeback story.

Setbacks can be a much-needed change in one's life, a course correction. However, you have to spend a little time licking wounds, and then immediately turn to looking up and forward and not get stuck in the past. And most importantly, you must resolve the mistakes made in your mind and move forward.

Core philosophy six is simply to plan for the unexpected and keep going. I always say, if you passed a burning building, you would not find 10 firemen standing in a huddle, pointing to each other, while the building was burning in the background, trying to find the culprit of the fire. We as human beings lose so much mental strength and time on trying to find the guy to hang on the cross or licking our own wounds when done wrong.

The story I just shared was a doozy. Most work fires that we deal with daily aren't that big, but still can completely throw a person off. I always say, *"Put the fire out; then after, circle back and figure out what happened."*

Why? Because when the fire is out, emotion wanes, logical thinking prevails. This is what we all need to do. We also need to wake up each day expecting fires instead of asking, *"I wonder if I will have a fire today?"*

Rather, ask yourself, *"When will the fire hit today?"* and *"How fast can I put it out and get back to productive work?"*

Top Sales people and the most successful people innately have characteristics that enable them to quickly fix things and

71

get right back to work. This is something you have to be cognizant of in order to hone the skill.

YOU are a fire fighter. We all are; but to be a great one, you need to understand your role in putting out the fire in the quickest and most efficient way. Many times, we do collateral damage in the process of a fire by being emotional, and in the end we still have a burned building to repair, and now have mounted more damage on top of the core issues.

Those people who master adversity strength, which is something I did not have come naturally to me in the start, are going to be viewed as the strongest leaders. I have been teaching this to people and observing people for decades now, successfully.

It is as simple as maintaining self-awareness. Catch yourself. Correct course. Be aware of where you are in the state of the problem. And help others correct course.

CHAPTER 12

Eight Core Philosophies for Success in Business Planning

Core Philosophy: Implement and Execute

ACCOUNTABILITY

YOU HAVE A PLAN NOW! You have considered all the aspects of that plan. You have written down the core philosophies that will help you excel, manage your time, stay on track, and succeed. But, what remains is the hardest part and interestingly the most likely intersection for failure.

The key to implementing your plan is first and foremost having a start date. You must pick a date to start your plan. If you are not of the mindset to make a big change and adapt to the daily tasks necessary to put the plan in place, I would rather you move the date back a little and commit 100% when you are ready. You will certainly fail if you start with a half heart.

At the same time, do not procrastinate. People who love the idea of embarking on a new way of life to greater success don't wait until winter or summer to get started. I realize we all do the mental start over in January only to see old habits form again by March. The standard of acceptable failure is very high in our society. New Year's resolution failures are at about 80%.

It is important to pick a good mental time of renewal. It may be a date that has significance to you or simply the most appropriate time, based on the goals and tasks involved in your plan. Some of my greatest plans in life started on odd dates. October sixth was one start date for me, a Sunday and a plan to lose 40 pounds. I did that by writing a blueprint for a plan that encompassed all I've written about in describing these philosophies. By writing down my greatest hurdles and obstacles, I identified foods with the highest calories and eliminated them for one year. To this day, several years later, I still am not consuming two of the five items on my 'can't eat' list: ice coffee and soda.

This book is clearly not a dieting book, yet life imitates life in so many aspects and I draw upon my own experiences to light your way. The most profound thing about setting my new weight goal and laying out the daily action steps to achieve it was coming to understand that I could not adapt some impossible fad diet that no one on earth could maintain.

I could not allow myself to fall to temptation. When you want to make real life long change, you put a goal in place and a path that is sustainable. I repeat, sustainable; NOT to be confused with obtainable. For example, I allowed myself a cheat day once per week. Not to be mistaken for total blow out days either. One day a week, instead of my healthy smaller meals, I allowed myself two small snacks and one anything goes meal plus desert of my choosing. I also prepared myself for cravings by having small portions of things I loved available. I learned to eat two squares of chocolate over the whole candy bar when I craved it.

Let me expand. I said early on your goals need to stretch you out of your comfort zone and that is true. It is more vital to miss a hard-fought goal and come close than to obtain or hit one that was mediocre.

The length of time you will take to get to any goal or plan will have no end if you do this right. It may have milestones where you see momentum and hit marks of preset, determined progress. And if the plan you put yourself on is life changing or career changing, then you will benefit the most from making those changes and that plan stick a lifetime.

My diet plan was not a diet and I have never called it such. I changed my eating plan. I got rid of all the pre-packaged, preservatives, and empty nutritional foods. I added new recipes that incorporated foods that support a healthy life style. I chose to introduce new things, including more organic foods and produce, into my daily eating plan. As a result, I traded calories for a better waist line, a better feeling, for better skin and hair. Of course, I also slowly added a work out plan that was pathetically simple to start.

This is my new life style, not a diet. I look different, I hit goals, I celebrated those goals when I hit them, and I did not give up when I hit plateaus of weight loss for months. I stayed the course, pushed myself harder, and kept my eye on the goal.

I have overcome many obstacles and I feel sometimes my life is one big example of adversity overcome by the triumph and determination of fighting my way back. I see things metaphorically. I see the lessons in experiences, and this probably comes from my deep inner spirit. I think we all have a spirit; that we all want to do well by ourselves and others, but along the way in life we are thrown off and find ourselves traveling a road we don't know how to get off, or how to turn back, or correct direction.

I have found myself down some dark and lonely roads that I was sure were leading to dead ends. I have walked roads for so long mired in solitude, thinking each step of the way that this is not the right road...this is not the right road.... Yet like a zombie, I kept putting one foot in front of the other, driving deeper in the wrong direction.

Our subconscious minds are far more powerful than we realize. The problem is we do not hear our minds as they do not speak audible words. They speak in silent thoughts. How we hear those thoughts, how we understand and translate them into action, determines how well we steer ourselves.

I do not have all the answers to life. I know my life is a journey of discovery and will be until the day I die. I hope each day to learn something new about the world, to slow down enough each day for moments, even if all I can spare is a moment, to look at the flowers growing outside my window, or the beauty of the humans around me. I hope each day to do well, to do right by others, and to stay on track, even as I know full well that I will be tempted to sway from the path most traveled.

I am a butterfly chaser and have been my whole life. The problem is the flight of the butterfly is temporary. When one flight dies, and you find yourself in unknown territories, surrounded by unfamiliar things, will you know your way back?

Will you forge a new path that is healthy, and that continues to take you where you intend to go? Will you be able to live with the fact you may never be able to get back to the road you were once on? And what if you left others walking down that path alone? What if you've had to watch some move on? Others who stopped, watched you wander away, but after a while had to stay on their own path?

The point is, do you have a path to begin with? Or are you right now in a field somewhere dreaming about the life you hope someone will hand you? If only you could be like X or Y. If only you could be so lucky. If only you could win the lottery. These are all things we all say about our dreams. The difference between the dream catcher and the rest of us is simply nothing at all. It's a plan that you implement and execute upon.

I had the hardest time recognizing the difference between a sayer and a doer. Sometimes people talk a good game; but as we all know, talk is cheap. In sales, it will always be about showing me the money.

I once had this manager who came to work early, worked late, was always first at the meeting, never forgot my birthday, and yet his results were poor, people didn't respect him, and I couldn't get his numbers up despite all my efforts.

In this case, I could not be *accountable* to his results. In the end, we are *accountable* to ourselves, but most of all, we have to deliver results. We must.

I will never brag; I will speak with wins and my sales numbers...then, if anyone challenges me, I can simply stand behind my own winnings as the proof of my pudding.

CHAPTER 13

Eight Core Philosophies for Success in Business Planning

Core Philosophy: Measurements of Success

INSPECT

MY GREATEST ADVICE TO MAKE these philosophies stick in business planning is to consistently and continuously measure your plan.

Inspect what you expect

I have heard over and over, and it is true. Often, we do not know in business how poorly a plan is going if we aren't measuring frequently. It is easy to be so focused on the day-to-day implementation and action steps that we lose sight of the future vision, our expectation of the new future that started us on this course. Conversely, without measurement, we also miss opportunities to celebrate and pause in reflection when a plan is working well. Measuring your plan will be key in both.

The three main ways that provide a true litmus test for our plan are simple yet often hard to do, as they require total self-awareness, and the willingness to look at, absorb, and then tweak your plan if you are off-track.

One: Measure your own progress against the prior month's progress.

Assuming you started your plan at the beginning of any given calendar month; you can stop and measure how you are progressing at the end of each month. Doing it in this block of time is smart. Like dieting, stepping on the scale daily can be discouraging, so a monthly measure allows you to step back and see your own progress. Make sure you have ways to measure your plan's progress. For instance, if there are metrics you can easily count to measure what you do daily, like time spent doing X or Y that lends to your financial betterment, then compare that to past months prior to having your plan in place. Are you prospecting more? Do you focus on what drives your bottom line? If you aren't sure, start journaling your daily activities to make that comparison.

I also suggest that you measure your ROI on time spent. In other words, are you getting a good return on the investment of your time? It may take a little while to see a return, but it truly is the measure of results from action.

If you are progressing from prior months, your activity level daily is more focused on what matters, makes money, makes production, gains results; then you get a PASS in this category (as this is a Pass/Fail kind of thing). We are all going to have off days, weeks...but months, no. I have been fortunate to find solace in my work despite whatever chaos surrounds me personally. Thus, it is my go to place for escaping my own head. I share this as I know many people like me who do not let life necessarily get in the way of work. The harder part for me was regulating work getting in the way of my life.

I am not suggesting more hours. Sometimes this is misinterpreted. We all need to work smart. Smarter doesn't equal more time; it equals more money-making hours within a week. I guarantee if you wrote down the top three time-suckers of your day to day work, it would either have a personal issue next to it, a personal distraction or a professional one, and may even have a person's name next to it.

How do you fix the time wasters? Well, write yourself a prescription to cure the ailment! Jot down on paper the time wasters. Once you see these habits and practices, you will recognize that you know the cure. You have the answers within you. We tend to look outward for answers because we aren't truly willing to look at ourselves. It takes honesty and strength to look at yourself. It takes getting out of your comfort zone. It takes introspection.

It is painful knowing a person is sabotaging their own career, or doing something off the mark consistently, and being, somehow, totally unaware. Don't be that person. This exercise of progress measurement, this process of you looking at you, is eye opening and fruitful. And necessary.

Two: Measuring results against the average of a team or peers:

This next measurement is key as much as the first. What is the water mark of your business? Is your nose above that line, or below it? Are you swimming like a pro or are you bobbing and gasping for air? Or worse, are you drowning? Do you know? Well, someone knows! First, your manager or your boss knows. They know if you're cutting it, staying up with the pack, or trailing. If you do not know, you are not truly looking at yourself for improvement or whether you are succeeding.

I understand not all of us want to be the top guy; we may be quite comfortable floating along in the middle of the pack. That is fine, of course, if that is an acceptable performance standard for your employer. All things in work and life can be measured. If you are on a team of people, in a branch of some sort, in an office amongst other offices in a region, or with a national company, you are able to measure against the averages.

Your manager should be sharing with you the performance measurements of your team in their weekly and monthly meetings. You then, knowing your own performance, can see what the average is of the team. Take a look at that and see where you stand. For all intents and purposes, measuring where you are helps to get you focused on where you are going. Measuring where you are amongst your peers, helps you see yourself as your boss does. It helps you recognize if you're pulling your weight.

Make no mistake, if you are below that line and a veteran at your job, somebody knows it. It is not a safe place to be. There are few employers who will carry the weight of an under-performer for long. If you find one of those places, then you probably should be more concerned about your entire job sovereignty than anything, as the leader that allows that, without guidance or assistance, is probably not in the right position.

Now, if you find you are *above average* then great. You are certainly doing many things right. You may even have a shot at the top of the pack if you desire that.

Three: Looking at the top performer on your team!

This is usually the easiest number or metric to find as it's typically highly celebrated by smart organizations and managers. On your team, you have a Number One person. More than likely, it's someone who is consistently there. More than likely, you're sick of hearing that person's name. That person, whether we like it or not, is doing many things right.

Not every person can do what the top person does. The best quarterback does not always make the best coach. Leadership is very different from leading the pack; although you can find people who are good at both, but not always! The best guy on your team is not necessarily the next person you should promote when the job requires leadership skills.

That said, the top person IS the person who you should be measuring your own numbers against, as they are doing a ton of things correctly. Learning the day-to-day best practices of the top performer can elevate an entire sales team. Measuring your own self against those numbers and how you stack up is also a good hard look in the mirror to what you are capable of doing, what you can achieve, and how someone on your team is getting it done right.

Also, and most importantly, to help clear away the excuses we give others and ourselves, there is this leadership rule called the Rule of One. I can't recall where I heard it first, but I have quoted it in leadership management for years. If ONE person on a given team can excel, then all can. Assuming that within a team the environment (e.g., sales markets, company, brand, working environment, culture, resources) is much the same for all, the Rule of One holds true: When one person breaks out of the pack on a sales team, that proves the capabilities of all.

Yes, it can be argued that top people are built of a certain DNA that innately propels them to success. Much of their skill, time, and attention focus on the right drivers to success and that is a road map that is imitated by others, once shared.

For managers who are leading sales, I always say, if you do not currently have a break out guy or gal, then hire one. One person who is set to excel within a team raises the bar for the entire team. Just as in shooting pool, you rise to your competition. Conversely, you are lowered or watered down by the opposite. When a team's average is low, it breeds lower standards. Find your superstar within your team and fan that flame; or go find a superstar to shake things up on your existing team.

The Action

IN THIS SECTION, I BEGIN TO BUILD upon the skills I want every top sales person to hone and the tactics that will make you excel and *See Your Way to Success*. The first chapter in this section might seem off-topic. Yet in truth, it's very much on topic, perhaps more so than any other in the entire book.

Gender should not matter. Gender does not matter. Gender does matter. Your opinion on this question? In truth, it is the reality that matters and how each of us chooses to believe and act when it comes to this potentially explosive topic.

"I'm damned if I do and damned if I don't. I might as well speak the truth. It is the truth that will be real when I am dying one day, and it will still be true 100 years from now when my son's grandchildren pick this up and want to learn about my life and career. So, here is my truth and best advice for up-and-coming women in business!"

~ C.B.

CHAPTER 14

The Female Phenom!

THE ELEPHANT IN THE ROOM

I MUST ADDRESS THE GROWING AND GREATEST quantity of questions I get, most of which come from women. In this chapter, I will speak from the heart the most raw and real advice to women I can offer.

I promise this doesn't come from a bitter or jealous place. I appreciate beauty and have experienced my share of the benefits society awards to those who are deemed physically attractive. Physical beauty will wane in time, a fact that catches many a beautiful woman by surprise. I knew this fact early on, so I didn't want to rely on my looks to get me places. I knew I needed tangible skills to sustain a life and career.

Beauty is based upon a WHOLE person, their inners and outers, if you will. One can decay the other and vice versa; truly I have seen the most esthetically beautiful people who are devoid of personality and character. Conversely some of the most awkward looking, less than perfect people have engaged me to my core with laughter, philosophical conversation, and intuitive, engaging discussion. These are deep souls and beautiful people inside.

I want to be taken seriously and have felt the need to prove my intelligence over and over, especially to women. I make the hair stand up on the backs of alpha women. I am left to calm, to reassure, to show them they can be the alpha, that it's OK to go ahead of me, that it is possible to befriend me, that in fact I welcome the relationship.

I am the alpha of all alpha females. I say this not because I earned that right or because I say it is so. I say this because God gave me a fearless ability to stand up against attacks. He made me confident in the most vulnerable of ways. In the fight of life, I come equipped with a mindset to win. When that trait is called on, my response goes to 100% auto pilot. This is a trait that I acknowledge gratefully. I have, literally and figuratively, been pounced on many times and have come to depend on my alpha qualities.

That said, I am not looking for fights from anyone. Just the opposite, I want to mentor women. I am now happy to be that person and as such, my approach is far less menacing to women. It helps that I am accomplished and established, so I am tested less often.

It is from this perspective, after three decades of playing the game, that I offer this chapter.

Women: like it or lump it; this is my truth, as I know it, and my best advice to you for success. If you are concerned with political correctness or a snappy, polished rhetoric to quote, it's not in this chapter. The next few pages are as raw as the world we strive to survive in every day.

Here's the elephant in the room. What role does my being female play in my success? Detriment? Opportunity? Inequality? What aspects of my career opportunities have been impacted by my gender?

There are books on this topic alone, and in truth, I could write a book on this topic myself. My experience is as a woman, living in a man's world, quite literally being the token female in a male dominated field, presents a challenge at every corner that I, and other women, must master.

We must not accentuate our femininity. We must not be viewed as a piece of ass. This may not be a popular opinion among either women or men. Yet it is a blunt truth that women in particular must embrace.

It takes extraordinary effort for a woman to be taken seriously, to have a respected voice, to be paid the same as our male counterparts. It can be exhausting to be a girl playing the game of survival and strategy on the same field as the boys. When it comes to femininity, the playing field is not necessarily equal, nor are the players.

I have seen incredibly talented women sabotage their own careers by sleeping around, or flirting, or emitting a sexual vibe in the work place. While I want to be viewed as an attractive, kept up, maintained, and healthy person, I never take it over the edge of sexually exploiting my looks. I consciously and deliberately manage my social media posts, my meetings, my travel, my voice, and my image.

I function under an umbrella that includes a distinct understanding that other women hate attractive women and men love them.

Are these truly the attitudes of all the men and women I work with? Hardly. This is the standard, however, that we pretend to be true. I live in a world where we must stay benign in that atmosphere, not shake up either side, not offend either side, and yet excel with both sides.

It is not a small task. I have learned to accept that, by the greater percentages, I am winning and I don't expect complete acceptance or love from either side. This is the philosophy and practice that works.

I can't live, operate, or manage to a 100% acceptance score. I have learned the hard way that will never happen. I learned, by watching dozens of women, how devastating it is to a person's career to sleep with a co-worker, boss, or senior leader. At the same time, I advanced my role. Am I so androgynous that I was over-looked by the goggling guys and their questionable advances?

No. The truth is I was hit on at every intersection by most men. The difference is I made a choice about my personal and professional morality. *I drew a line between what my career means as it relates to inter-work relations and I remain at all times on my side of that line.*

It was, and is, difficult at times to do so without coming off as prudish or becoming water to the oil of the men's club. I have succeeded by understanding how men are; by appreciating the fact my relationship with male counterparts is strictly business and friendship, and of course by acting unfazed by all of it. Thus, I was neither a threat nor a prospect. I earned respect in the board room even if there were those who desired me in the bedroom. I kept those bedroom thoughts only thoughts to maintain my respect levels.

I still see women who make these crucial mistakes. Instead of dating outside the pool of work, they date within it. They may never know how these practices damn them. I am certain if they knew beforehand, they would reconsider. It is my hope to help women avoid mistakes of this type that can define their futures at work.

I have adopted a man's attitude. If the women are careless enough to play this game, then they need to accept the repercussions. Sadly, many of them don't have the experience or wisdom to understand the price tag this places on their long-term careers. For some brilliant women, I have seen that price be quite hefty.

Today I am a female mentor to women across the nation. I am not a proponent of women's liberation. I do not believe that I deserve extra opportunity or chances. I am not in favor of giving women less stringent requirements to hold a position at the board room table.

I have seen that I must work extra hard to get to that table. I must out sell my peers and have results greater than my peers. I have to maintain excellence at all times, and I have to be a clear front runner to NOT be ignored or over-looked for advancement.

That said, I can help women by showing them how to put down their signs for equal rights and learn what it takes to go to work and surpass the competition, no matter the gender.

Work hard, be an example for other women, do what is right, shine in the work place through action and results. Expect nothing more or less than your male counterparts and demand respect if you have earned it.

Don't ask to play from the women's tee, step up and grab some iron and show them what you're made of. I don't need to be equal to men, because in many cases, I am greater than my male counterparts.

That is not something I feel the need to brag about, it just is what it is. In many other cases I am not as good as my male counterparts. I admit that. I just am good enough to live in the world I chose to reside in. I chose this path, this career, nobody owes me anything.

It's sad to me when I see men who think old school, who clearly objectify women as lessor, who subconsciously are discriminative without even knowing it in fact, because they were brought up in a generation or an ethnicity that has taught them this.

I also don't think I am physically equal to men, nor do I want to be. I am good with them having their own clubs and I like my own female clubs. I think it's ok for them to do things only men do and I think the same for women.

I don't want to live in a world personally that is made up of political correctness. I would die in that world. I am not perfect, nor is my male counterpart, but I am for certain going to fight for my right as a PERSON.

When I lay down the work and you short me because of being female, I will rise up against that.

Men: I applaud you for having read to this point. The lesson I hope you will see here is how to stay out of my (and other women's) cross hairs on this topic. I promise that if I am undermined by any person, I will call out such action just the same if I am disrespected.

Women and Men: Understand there are inequalities still, yet embrace where we reside and help us push that evolution forward through the example of hard work and earned promotions, rather than yelling the loudest or making threats to gain your piece of the pie.

And please, please do not ask anyone why you lost your promotion, your popularity, or respect if you chose to mix your personal life and work life in such a manner that it deterred you from getting your due in the office, even if you actually put up a great work ethic, have a sharp mind, and deliver proven results. If all of that is undermined by the naked photo you sent to the boss who circulated it then to every other manager, who then looked at you in the meeting you were conducting like a picture out of his favorite porn magazine, then who is to blame here for that perception?

Yes, there is a double standard. No one will recall what the guys did last week to whom or with whom. The only way we can impact that standard is to be part of the power structure within. The sooner you accept it and face it, the better you will be. The better example you set within the work place, the better all women will be. I believe it is something we should all strive for.

This is not to say I have not struggled in my career with these facts. I have also not ignored them. I have been at a very low place mentally at times realizing the deficits of female verses male dominance in the work place. I have cried many times privately realizing that no matter how hard I work, just because I am female, accolades will come far harder. I've been the butt of jokes that got back to me. I've been ignored in meetings when I spoke, only to hear my same point made and revered by others. It hurts knowing that my opinion may be less respected.

These societal standards, the innate discriminations embedded in the mindsets of a professional culture, are so subtle it's hard to point out at times. Rather than fight a riptide that at times has knocked me to my knees, I choose to swim hard along the rip current, find the break in the tide, and then fight my way to shore.

I become angry about it at times and choose to put that anger towards insurmountable success. Undeniable success. That demands, in and of itself, acknowledgement. Those victories have given me faith that while not all women are as persistent or stubborn as I may be, it is possible. Anything is possible when you set your mind to it.

Obstacles strengthen my resolve. In hindsight, even those times when I bewailed the inequities my gender forced upon my career, these obstacles have made me wiser to future discrepancies. Yes, it is hard to not become hardened by these things; it is challenging to remain unemotional toward those who overlook your challenging work, or who privately denounce you for no other good reason than being a woman in a predominantly male club.

I have allowed myself two things to handle the really prominent biases.

One, I call them out when I see them with certainty and two, I address the issues head on and unofficially. Meaning, I don't report interactions I feel are done with bias when I am able to resolve the issue directly.

To be clear, I am not saying that I would ignore physical violation. I am saying that I choose to handle my personal, professional battles head on, mano a mano.

This may seem confrontational. In reality, it leads to trust and loyalty. When people speak behind people's backs, which I can say I have also done at times, it doesn't lend to growth or healing; it cracks the foundation of trust between individuals.

I wish more people understood how damaging that sort of behavior is. I would rather have someone mad at me directly than hurt me indirectly. When trust is broken, that is the gift that keeps on hurting and it will eventually erode a relationship to the point of no return. Experience has taught me the value in trusting people, to give an individual the opportunity to understand me directly. Once out in the open and in conversation, the issue can be dealt with, allowing us to move forward with at least the respect and trust levels intact.

I know I work harder than most, have better results than most, and deliver greater more caring leadership. Because of this confidence, I am not shy to look a man right in the face and say, someone might call X discrimination and let that settle. The problem often fixes itself.

I have taken the high road more often than not. Battled the bias with my work and allowed that to have a voice that conquers anything else. It is hard not to become bitter or defensive when you live in a world like this day in and day out. My true inner strength to rise above this in my career has come from the belief that Karma and God will take care of me; that those who do wrong to others will pay a price at some point; that those people less genuine will be seen as such.

In my heart, I care for everyone I work with, even those who aren't good to me. THAT is my beacon. That is what carries me through with a resolve that what I have given will come back to me tenfold even if it's hard to see at times. It always has and I believe that it always will.

And alas, after 30 years in the boy's club, I wouldn't want to be anywhere else! Believe it, or not. I have a thick skin, a deep sense of humor, a callus but nurturing leadership style, and I also have lifelong friends as men who have proven to be more loyal in the friendship zone than anywhere else in their lives. This may seem contradictory to some of what I say above. But the truth is, I am a tom boy to a large degree. The things I like to talk about, sports, motorcycles, current news or the ribbing and the funny humor are things I migrate to. If you put me in a room filled with a hundred people, I would not naturally head to the women. I would most likely be found sitting back with the guys.

I also am somewhat rare I guess, in that I see the world often through the eyes of a man; and while I know what I have written is blunt, it is as real as it can be to say to other women, if you truly have the guts for it, you can live here happily.

The only times I have not been truly and genuinely happy is when a man is threatened by me and decides to treat me poorly. I will not do well in that environment and sadly that has happened repeatedly in my career. I try so hard for it not to happen, I tone down my very loud demeanor, and try to take the second seat; but something in me rises up and my quest for success prevails, can't be stifled, can't be silenced or hidden. In the end, when my team can see that in me lies the strength of a warrior, and that I am loyal to the end, that I am with them to the end, they will always have my back. And when they don't, the gloves will most certainly come off.

I have known for a long time that I must work harder to put lady professionals at ease when I enter a room. The other phenomenon about women is they don't trust each other. Think about it. Women are hurt by other women in relationships through their male or female partners. I make an effort to let women know I am one of them. I am with them. I am for them. Because I am.

I am who I am. I like what I like. I wouldn't choose to change anything, not where I am, or how I got here. Not even the horrible obstacles or lowest moments, because the mountains I have climbed have rendered beautiful journeys, happy endings, and glorious views.

I don't know when I will stop climbing. I am not sure anyone ever does. I think as people we pause at times to check out the view, sit back, and reflect on how far we've come. For me, climbing is what keeps me alive. Knowing there is more life to see, conquer, and experience keeps me moving forward. The view is already great where I am, but I think I will keep going higher...and see if there is even more to see!

To all the ladies who are seeking more in their careers, I say strike with the same professionalism we are asking of our male counterparts. Be the example of women who come and conquer with great results, be fearless, be brave, be determined, and most of all, do not be afraid or even insecure about who you are.

You are going to get teased, laughed at, pushed down, hit on, objectified, diminished, discarded, and discriminated against, however justified or subtle that it may be presented. You will know all of this is happening when it's happening. You will have a choice to rise above it, stay the ground and keep it moving, or stop and fight for your principles.

Pick your battles as you lose pace and whether you like this or not, companies don't want to hear it, they fear it in fact. So, by going along to a large degree you are proving your ability to withstand. I could have seen myself the victim many times, and sometimes I asked myself why I didn't just file lawsuits against all the wrong doings; by now I could be sitting in the farm house somewhere, making my favorite jam, and writing love stories while I take naps and run in the middle of the day. Instead, I am out here in the battle and loving it.

I believe in the fight I am in. I feel I am making more a difference where I am than taking up some legal battle that labels me a mole. No, I'm going to take the high road, and I'm gonna keep climbing. I will deal with the obstacles as they come, one by one, as always. I hope to always project an amazing image to my subordinates.

I love women professionals. I know formidable women who are not messing up their careers by being promiscuous. I have seen women withstand a lot, and it's hard for me to tell another woman to be strong when I know something unfair is happening. That said, I also teach them my tactics for dealing with it. I would much rather make a person shrink, looking him in the eye, than talk around that person.

So, ladies, fight a smart fight. There is a lot of pie to go around if you can be brave and smart and work hard. I know you will each find your way, the way you know how; but the truth is, times are changing, and we are going to be witness to a continued evolution. We now represent over 53% of the business world, for the first time in history. Much change will continue. We are strong in numbers, finally.

"Your life does not get better by chance, it gets better by change."

~ Jim Rohn

CHAPTER 15

Swipe Right! Is Your Employer a Match?

HOW TO HAVE AND CONTROL HEALTHY EMPLOYEE ATTRITION AND SATISFACTION

IF THE MORTGAGE INDUSTRY WAS a dating service, it would have been out of business decades ago. Neither employer nor employee gets it right.

Imagine if both sides had to complete a match survey. What would it look like?

Would YOU be with the right employer when it was all done? Or would you have realized you belong somewhere else?

How many of you are unhappy where you are but think there is no solution?

In the 30 years plus since my first banking job as a Teller (shortly after I graduated high school), I have switched jobs four times; which is quite incredible in an industry that sees 40% attrition annualized. Yes, I've worked for companies that were purchased by other companies, and been through mergers, acquisitions, takeovers, and bail outs. But, as far as me resigning and seeking alternate employment, that has only happened four times.

Was this a plan? Yes and no. Most career-minded people do not go looking for that ultimate long-term match, not really. Think about it, have you given thought to your perfect job? Employer? Industry? Have you taken the time to identify the match that could last a lifetime?

Most Mortgage Loan Originators may look to settle down, per se, but they aren't really in it for the long haul. They are in it for as long as they are making good and quick money. That starts out of the gates with requests for lucrative sign on bonuses and upfront guarantees. Yes, here comes the parade of semi productive originators with production reports in tow like a diary or photo album for their profile, and anxious mortgage companies who don't dig deep enough and are more than happy to write checks from their CEO's check books, just to say they won the hiring bid. And six months later, when the guarantee runs out, their winners can't sustain originator income on their own sales platform. Sound familiar? I hope not, but it's an all too familiar story.

Through that process of loyalty and longevity when I outlasted well past my peer's tenure on average, what I discovered was a recipe for success and job advancement. I've written seminars on this topic; not just my own success and how I came to get it right so often and for so long, but also in understanding why I stayed, and then helped replicate an environment for my employers that would lead a sales force to emulate the same loyalty. I'm proud to say I've accomplished this on both sides of the fence for myself and for the companies whose sales force I have helped lead. So, let me share with you some success techniques on this topic that will put money directly back into your pockets.

It's Not a Fairy Tale, but Happily Ever After Can Happen

To be clear, I am not out to convince you to stay where you are currently employed. Or to move. The point is to find out where you truly belong and get it right either now or next time. I made a career mistake early on by having tunnel vision about my first job change. My then national employer didn't have B paper mortgage product, and I had a territory that was mainly all B & C paper. Clearly, I was not a match at all to my employer. This mismatch came about from a series of acquisitions that left me seven years into the job and suddenly a fish out of water. Pun intended. I realized the mismatch when I consistently had to turn over business referrals to my competition, referrals that came from long sought-after networks. My employer had changed direction, and I was not equipped, or interested, in following.

I started dating and eventually made a move. It took a year of dating potential employer suitors. In hindsight, I realized I spent all my interview time making sure that the place I would go would solve my biggest and current problem. The only issue with this process and mentality is that mortgage lending is complex, and you must examine and vet all applicable areas of your product, price, and personal benefits. The end of the story here is simply that I got my B & C paper lender for a price tag of horrible processing and service that I had to compensate for. So, the trade up for more applications was a greater fall out after the point of sale. The net difference was a wash; except in this scenario, I had started to earn a reputation with my current referral partners for not having great service. Thankfully, I assessed my situation quickly, and made another move in under two years that landed at my next 13-year job.

Due diligence is, of course, a no brainer. Finding your match, finding your happily ever after is so much more than due diligence. Whether you are the employer or employee, the same theory applies. I advise against quick hiring to fill a quota or head count.

Employers: While we all have a business plan to meet, I would argue all day, that to avoid attrition, which my company AnnieMac has done excellently, and at 1/3 the national attrition rate, you must create an environment and culture that creates a working atmosphere that includes investment into your employees, such as: family, life and work balance, recognition, onboarding and orientation support, and career succession with personal professional development. You must also differentiate yourself, and you must understand who you are, on both sides.

Employees: For that match to occur you need to know what you want to represent, how you want to feel every day, what is in it for you; but also what you bring to the table. Are you looking for your *Happily Ever After* mortgage company? If you think that's a fairy tale, it's not. Mortgage Originators need to understand when seeking their *Happily Ever After Employer* that they need to fall in love. They also need to not expect perfection, and they need to understand what they stand to lose by pond hopping.

We have become a society of quitters. There is a lot to be gained by sticking with your employer in tough times and vice versa, I will add. Many times, I have seen the ranks of my peers fleeing over rate hikes or product restriction to the next company when it was an industry or market reaction, and I always felt sad for them. I knew they were chasing a ghost. They didn't like the impending changes of their current employer.

When I came to AnnieMac 11 years ago, I was actively seeking my *Happily Ever After Employer*. My prior company, who I would probably still be working for today, had closed its doors during the mortgage industry implosion. When I sought a new employer, I did so with eyes wide open. I had opportunities to go to bigger companies, but I had the foresight to realize those companies would have to shrink. Today my company is bigger than many of those companies I passed over. I left one place where I was literally the last man standing amongst hundreds of national sales associates. I both wanted and needed to get it right, and I am happy to report that I did.

I will go ahead and state the obvious, with me being female, looking for executive or senior level sales management jobs was a bit difficult and disheartening. But, as it goes, lightning does strike twice. I found my way to a growing employer, who knew my value, and whose culture was truly a match for me. They were the new and improved lender to replace the dying breed of lenders who could not evolve quickly enough. They were innovative, classy, and most of all, fun and funny. They were the new kid in the ghost town, and they were here to rebuild. They had and still have a value proposition that is a niche. They have differentiated, persevered, evolved, and adjusted to market speed bumps. They've also grown, pragmatically at times, and fast when there was market share to be easily gained. They have stayed on the edge of technology while staying current and relative and human.

If you are an employer seeking Happily Ever After Mortgage Originators, then look for the guys and gals who match your culture. But you must first understand who you truly are, and you must represent yourself as that in truth. I will add you have more to win on a gut feeling than you do sometimes on vetted production. What one guy does at his old shop will not guarantee success at your shop. Also, don't write big checks unless you can sustain that originators income with product, price, support, and business after their guarantee dries up. They will not stay if they can't sustain it with the normal sales platform offered. I see many large mortgage companies whose attrition rate is ridiculous at the four to six-month mark; I want to invite myself to one of their board meetings.

If you are a Mortgage Originator seeking employment, question and beware of the upfront guarantee. A lot of times those blind dates are a killer. If you are a mortgage originator, and you are seeking a Happily Ever After Employer, then look for the company whose culture is your match. Who are you falling in love with? Yes, they need to have product, price, and differentiation, but most of all look around their castle:

- Are their current employees happy?
- What do you see on social media about that company?
- Any awards they've won for employment satisfaction?
- Are the employees a family?
- Are they working as a team?
- What is their reward program?

If you get your match right, your career will thrive and your referral partners will gain confidence in you, every passing year. Trust me. Your career succession will experience momentum that is greater than your peers who pond hop. Loyalty and longevity are understated values.

This business is a grind. Relationships are work. We all know it. However, if you get your match right on either side, in hiring or being hired, everyone wins. There is a very large price tag for the turn over that is going un-analyzed. Nobody should pond hop for reasons that are not substantial. That said, what we all deem substantial, varies. I put your happiness, stress level, and work life balance at the top.

There are Happily Ever After Employers out here...just ask me!

"Above all, be the hero of your life, not the victim."

~ Nora Ephron

CHAPTER 16

What Kind of Sales Person Are You?

PERSONALITY QUIRKS HELP SALES PEOPLE EXCEL

WE ALL KNOW SOMEONE WHOSE DESK IS READY for a photo shoot at any moment. You know who you are!

We know amongst our teams, who has the Type A personality, who is High Detail and who is not, and who has full blown OCD. We know who the most impatient people on our teams are and which people exercise emotional intelligence or lack the ability to do so. We know who is hyper active and who operates seemingly with super powers.

Personality quirks offer a good compass, if read right in hiring, to guide the selection of a sales person who can become your next super star. Sales is a tough gig. It is not for the thin skinned. Sales people are drawn to the control they have in structuring their own work days and not punching a time clock or exist on someone else time table. Sales draws people to it who can be burned and churned and will withstand the storm of a market that is forever evolving. Never has that been truer than today and for the sales soldiers who survived the past decade.

One of the greatest traits of the most successful sales people is Impatience. Impatient people are drawn to sales, believe it or not, because they are driven by a sense of urgency that they must control. Impatient people act fast, they want answers quickly, and they react faster than a patient person. These characteristics lend greatly to excellent customer service.

The challenge for an impatient sales person is managing the sense of urgency. I learned early on in my management career that most of my staff in sales were impatient. Rather than fight against it or look for and hire more patient people, I accepted it. Had I looked for patient people I would have staffed myself with sales people whose lack of urgency would have led to poor sales results.

Many companies are diligently using personality indexing these days, so they can find the impatient sales people and put them behind a desk, and on a phone, and set them free to run at their goals.

Hyperactivity is another stigma-related personality characteristic that makes a great sales person. Some days a hyper sales person will do the work of two! These people by nature require less sleep, are always in motion, and tend to be better doers and networkers. Often, they are also gym enthusiasts who, if managed properly, are simply moving at a faster pace than most.

As for managing hyperactive people, it is important to drive them to goals so that they can manage that hyperactive personality with some measurable daily and weekly milestones. Otherwise you may end up with a lot of motion but little results.

I am a hyperactive person, and I require less stimulation to remain at a consistent high-level pace and often out last my competition if not out work them. Hyperactive people have endurance and that is something that wins in sales.

At one time, hiring sales folks labeled with OCD, or even a layman with the less serious label of a Type A personality, was discouraged by sales managers. I worked for many years for a company who would use their personality indexes to push their Type A's into operational positions, where multitasking and management of 50-60 mortgage files required an organized individual. That thought process changed over time when less organized sales people proved to not be the best at customer service or sales tasks, which arguably require organization at the highest level. This is especially true today with the new originators who must remain licensed and educated, serving multiple professionals in purchase transactions, realtors and attorneys, and savvy millennials. Where once the Type A was rare in sales, you will now find more Type A's excelling in sales than ever before.

I am an OCD person and Type A person to the hundredth degree. People discouraged me early on when I was in my young twenties about becoming a Loan Officer. I started in the mortgage industry as a processor and had a reputation for hitting deadlines, handling large pipelines, and multi-tasking with detail. Nobody wanted to see me leave that role and especially my loan officers who I faithfully served. When I made the change over to sales, I was told that my personality would not lend to sales. Clearly, they were wrong, as evidenced by my successful sales career.

Having a Type A mind allows me to funnel more leads in a more organized fashion and also allows me to easily handle the complexity of a mortgage transaction. My ability to make organization from chaos helps me keep the many details of my client's financial picture in perspective and also absorb the massive guideline details that are constantly evolving. Today, I no longer hide that this is who I am, it has served me very well.

These semi controversial personality characteristics have served me and many of my successful sales people well. Personality indexing is something that can help any company find the right people and it should be used by those managers who aren't looking for the perfect person. Quite frankly, the patient, middle of the road organizational person who doesn't show signs of some level of high energy, is probably a great person to pass on.

I would also add that understanding YOUR OWN personality plays a big part in finding the right company, one that also gets the value of this concept. Finally, knowing this upfront can lend greatly to proper management by a seasoned manager who knows how to bring the very best out of you.

The very last tip I will give to sales managers is that you need to distinguish between *passion* and *emotion*. It can look like the same thing. Sales people are passionate by nature; and those who are highly engaged and invested in your company, will be the same people who react with the loudest voice when they see something they don't like. Now, I am not making excuses for poor behavior. Every sales person is obligated to show Emotional Intelligence. However, don't put the fire your sales person has out, because you mistake their passion for emotion, and you accidentally extinguish it trying to push back on that passion. It can lead to a lot of unhappy sales people who ultimately may leave your company for another company that *gets them*. In the end, you never know when that other company might fan the flames of that passion, because they understand it for what it genuinely is.

The definition of rhetoric is: All Talk. No Action. The opposite is a quote I love from Will Rogers:

"Even if you are on the right track, you'll get run over if you just sit there."

CHAPTER 17

The Lost Art of Execution

REINVENT A SUCCESSFUL WORK ETH-IC

IT TOOK ME MANY YEARS TO REALIZE that people, by and large, are not doers. People disappoint when you are a teacher, as anyone who coaches, teaches, and trains will agree. There are clichés like, *You can lead a horse to water but you can't make them drink*, that demonstrate my point. These phrases exist because they are excuses repeated often by failing managers.

I have spent my entire life applying tricks and traits to get the horses to the water and make them drink; this despite the depressing fact that the statistical learning rate of the average person is 40%!

The greatest trait I would credit to my own teaching success is that I am a doer. I apply the same process to my trainings as I do to everything else I do. When my class has ended, my work has not. I review my speech and reflect on the message just delivered. My own training happens after class as I check in periodically and consistently to *Inspect what I Expect!*

This is the number one tip I can offer to any leader: *Inspect what you expect.* Sounds stupidly simple. It is by far, the lesson most often forgotten by managers and leaders alike. It is also never missed by seriously successful leaders.

Do not make the mistake of poo-pooing this idea by confusing it with micromanagement. I am not a proponent of adult leadership turned into babysitting. People who are treated as adults and offered a process to follow that provides measurable growth and positive results, do respond appropriately to embrace new challenges and concepts.

To inspect what you expect is not micro management. No one invests in something they expect returns on without a daily monitoring—except when it comes to human behavior. Think about this. Can you name someone who enrolls, implements, and stipulates change without a desired outcome?

A remarkable story that demonstrates this came out of the imploding mortgage industry in 2007. AnnieMac had to shift gears as did all other companies. I was tasked to lead the charge on our core value proposition in a new model, Realtor Partnership curriculum and technology. At the time, we adapted this differentiator; it was being offered to other lenders as well. For two years, we were one of a small group of lenders in a race to create elite offerings, at a time when real estate was being punished by the crimes of our past. And then there was one. We found ourselves alone in the field as the only lender getting real, tangible results with this program.

Why? Execution. We had put the tool in place and implemented a training program and a help desk. We escalated visibility of the program in all departments, in recruiting and sales, as well as retention. We made this program top of mind and from this base, grew our (then minimal) purchase platform to tens of thousands of realtor affiliations, all while watching our competition die on the vine. This program failed for all six of our competitors.

Inspect what you Expect!

Today I see young, new originators jumping into this industry who are eager to learn. They are attracted by our robust education system and on-boarding. Our company helps them learn today's products and systems while addressing philosophical mindsets, emotional intelligence, and change.

Every part of the process is measured, and all is inspected. While we still see people occasionally fail, our retention rate is far higher than our competition and so is our time to production. In fact, we have doubled the production of our sales force 80% of the time in under 18 months. Why? Execution of our program implementation.

To be the very best, you must:

- Apply what you learn
- Act on the notes you write during class and in work
- Measure what you are doing, regularly
- Practice what is new until it becomes innate.

If you are a leader, you must:

- Ensure you have your team's attention; if they don't show up for training, they won't learn

- Deliver amazing training and shared knowledge

- Implement follow up inspections to measure the execution success of every person

- Verbalize the expectation

- Follow through

Finally, I find that if you want your troops to shovel harder, you must grab a shovel yourself. Too many leaders let authority go to their heads. They sit in their plush seats in their Ivory towers and bark down orders to a fleet that cannot flank right as asked without casualty and the reaction of your troops is defiance because they see the leadership as out of touch. The very best way to get that fleet to attack that hill is to place yourself amongst them and run shoulder to shoulder at the hill. You will be more relatable. You will be more believable and most of all, you will give applicable and relevant guidance from the ground.

To *Inspect what you Expect*, set up at least three check points where you measure, in tangible terms, the results of a project, performance, or production. Motivate your subordinates to participate and to expect inspections after they leave the classroom, or the change is implemented. Coach from the field not the sideline. Be relevant. Earn respect through integrity and hard work.

Leadership is earned not rewarded. Management is a job; but Leadership is a responsibility and an honor.

"You must master a new way to think before you can master a new way to be."

~ Marianne Williamson

- Defense of why and justification that what we are currently doing is working

- Reluctance to waste time doing what's necessary until the change is complete and we get into a mindset to accept and adhere to the change.

Reluctance, Defense, Time Wasted = Initial Change Reaction.

I am quite normal and resist change as we all do. And yet, I also help people learn to embrace change, to prepare for those intersections in time where a change is needed, and to develop the personality traits to ease resistance. When I teach on this topic, it truly helps individuals, managers, and entire organizations to successfully minimize the impact and losses that are the fallout of *Change Resistance*.

When you look to the most successful people in the world, you will find individuals who embrace change, who evolve, who study what is current, who actively move their chess pieces, and who are constantly assessing. The same is true for companies that can evolve.

I truly believe one of the reasons I have succeeded in life is confidence in my ability to adapt. When I was a young girl, I was not seasoned in life with experiences many take for granted. For instance, as a young adult, I did not know how to behave going to a restaurant. In that atmosphere, I watched silently and mimicked what I saw. When I got a job, I did the same. When I moved to a new place, I again followed the same practice.

Watch. Assess. Learn. And change as needed. This is how I related to people when I became a mortgage loan officer as well. This ability to blend into a world where, in my mind, I did not fit, is a skill that I have honed, a skill that propels me each time I call upon it.

Conversely, I think people fail or struggle when they are unwilling to change. Fighting against change rather than owning it results in their world evolving, often beyond them, until they become irrelevant or disconnected and unable to excel.

Thirty years in the Mortgage Industry has taught me one paramount thing: that the market is constantly evolving and changing. We sell on a moving platform. Obviously, rates fluctuate, markets expand and contract, guidelines become stricter and then relax. Essentially, we control very little from the sales seats of our mortgage companies when it comes to the winds that are put in our sails.

Mortgage professionals, who get that we are an extension of Wall Street fluctuations, economic effect, and industry reaction to both, spend less time focused on metrics (which are better monitored by the experts in their companies and executive teams), and more time focused on their own hours every week in prospecting and working on actual sales.

Having been the teacher and motivator for sales forces for nearly two decades and direct mortgage sales for almost 30, I can assure you, top producers who are excelling are individuals who pay less mind to the things out of their control and more mind to the things they directly affect, such as:

- How many referral partners they touch,

- How many families they help,

- The level of service they provide,

- The hours spent focused on money making tasks rather than distractions that will upend any sales person.

The bulk of your time as a sales professional must advance the funnel you create for sales flow to make new, lucrative relationships. Those who serve their clients excellently, and who perform the proper networking tasks that keep sales thriving, growing, and referring, are the people who will end up on the winning side of the fence.

I have watched over both successful and failing sales people. I have lead many under dog teams and companies to sales success through creating an unobstructed vision to what they control and by keeping them from sitting like a deer in head lights when difficult changes occur. Accept necessary change when the industry demands it. The quicker a sales executive team can get their sales force into the mindset of change, perhaps through powerful trainings such as Emotional Intelligence and Change Management, the quicker their sales folks will rise above the challenges.

How do I know this? Because, despite closing a national company in 2007; literally being the last person standing in a national retail company that was in 14 major markets and that left hundreds of sales folks scrambling for new employment, I never lost faith that I would find the high ground. I led my sales people to avoid the pond hopping out of the industry that so many folks did over the last decade. I led my people to a safe and growing company that could remain focused on the future of our current market.

Without giving away any of my current company sales strategies, the greatest advice I can give any executive or senior level sales leaders is keep your sales force pliable, flexible, and focused. Yes, I personally experienced the highs and lows that the industry relentlessly dished out in the past decade, but I avoided hitting rock bottom and helped hundreds of others avoid it, by helping them focus on where they controlled their own destinies and left the vision and economic paths and strategies to my CEO and to other subject matter experts.

That said, while I've been in boats that were taking on water, I always kept a bucket in my own hand; and when I was yelling bail to my sales teams, I was bailing at the same rate. In the end, sales leadership is about clearing and uncluttering the complex atmosphere of our sales environments and keeping the team focused on the tasks they control.

Ask anyone who is truly successful, and you will either find an intentional person who is focused on the daily sales task that expands their funnel of referral partners, prospecting, and ultimately delivering a superior service experience to their clients. When you look around and find a bunch of sales people focused on rate and product and market flux, expect to be handed those excuses as to why their sales are unremarkable. A successful sales team is one who finds the wave and rides long and wide rather than one who simply rides the wave straight in to lap against the shore.

"It is when you're going through the most difficult chapter of life that your hero is revealed, and how beautiful it is when you finally realize you have the strength to save yourself."

~ Dodinsky

CHAPTER 19

Give Yourself a Raise

FAST FIVE

MOTIVATION COMES IN DIFFERENT drivers. We are driven by many things. We know what they are as all sales people pray to a handful of common ones which include but aren't exclusive to:

- Recognition
- Reward
- Legacy

- Competitiveness

- Security

- Wealth

- Family

When top sales people are surveyed, they will most commonly say that they want recognition more than anything and that they gain a sense of pride from being at the top. However, every person who enters sales does so with the idea of getting rich quick. Those who truly rise to the tops of their sales field are the ones who will tell you there are no short cuts to success. There are a lot of distractions, hiccups, speed bumps, and plenty to derail you on the road to the pot of gold. Often, weak workers enter sales with the idea of flexible schedules and end up broke.

I have been managing and leading top sales people for three decades and am a winning sales person myself, a decorated veteran. Early on, I was told by a great mentor to come from a genuine place and I would always make a lot of money. I have learned this is a true statement. While I am a fierce competitor, the whole money thing is a secondary perk. My main motivator is helping others.

I could write a library full of books about great sales guys who don't do well due to the obvious distractions. Instead, I will make this simple. When we are in a drought of any kind, a market shift, a rate hike, a dry spell, we tend to over think our way through it, create further complexities, and end up back to the basics before we are done.

GREAT sales guys do not vary from their paths. Like the proverbial tortoise and the hare racing, they are the tortoise; steady as they go, consistent. And that consistency pays huge dividends.

Fastest Five Ways to Give Yourself a Raise

1. Assess your daily activities: Make sure 75% of your weekly hours are spent on sales prospecting efforts: Marketing, Sales Meetings, Sales Calls, Sales Quotes, Sales applications, Sales referral Meetings. Do NOT sit on your horrible pipeline like you are laying the golden egg. You can't excel if you are too busy counting the pennies in your wallet. Yes, manage your pipeline effectively with great service; but do not obsess. Pay attention to this. You can meet 75% in many ways; you can have all sales days and half sales days, but when it adds up at the end of the week, it needs to be 75%. Great sales guys do this automatically and innately.

2. Vet your referral partners: How many of you are spending time trying to get business where the well is dry? The first guy or girl who approaches you at the networking event is sure to be the one who has the least business: Happy to be there for the free appetizers and cocktails, hoping to make affiliations, and usually has few loyalties to anyone.

   The top producers are already in bed with someone and do you know what top sales guys and gals think about that? They don't care! In fact, they do their homework before they network to find their target referral partners, not avoid them. They find the big hitters and they say, 'So what?' to the idea of competition.

   Top sales people go after a piece of the pie. They innately understand that every relationship is either growing or waning, and they take their chances on getting a foothold, and then working their way in from there, understanding their competitor's strategy and playing against it, subtly. In short, they find the prize and they go for it. They aren't excuse makers or afraid.

3. BELIEVE in What You are Selling: Show me a guy using a script and I will show you a guy whose phone is being hung up on frequently. Nobody wants to talk to that guy. Or the corny one-liners that they try to keep customers on the phone with.

    Top sales guys are winning because they approach their consumer intelligently, confidently, and with solutions in mind. Their product is solving a problem and they get to work on finding that problem and solving it, as quickly as possible, while gaining trust through intelligent statements. They are also great listeners and they NEVER OVER SELL. I really dislike the guy who goes on just to hear himself speak. When it's sold, pull the trigger, set the gun down. Sure, do a happy dance, then, take a seat. When you believe in what you are selling, it comes through. When you aren't sure that comes through as well. Notate!

4. Act, Look, and Speak Professionally. I know a lot of hood sales guys. Yes, I said hood. I love them all, so no offense. We all come from different back grounds and trust me; I am not a silver spoon girl. That said, people want to buy from someone who makes them feel they made an educated choice, not a guy with hair do like the *Flock of Seagulls* and the crack of his ass showing through torn jeans that are being held up by boxer briefs. I don't care if your job is 80% telephony either. Dress for success. Trust me on this. Yes, I dress down at times, but even then, if I were surprised by a customer, I would not be out of place. Think about that. Also, ladies, stop dressing like you are about to be photographed for Playboy. I realize for some, it's hard to down play the

beauty; that said, keep it clean and professional, you will not be taken seriously otherwise; trust me on this. You can be beautiful while dressing sharp and professional.

5. This is a Contact Sport! You can't hide behind your telephone if you're a top producer. Top producers are everywhere. I used to wonder how top producers could be at the networking events, doing radio, TV, social media, and meetings and still have top numbers. It's because they understand their name is their brand, their company is their brand, and it's vital to be SEEN more than heard. They also usually have a team of people helping them.

I realize most companies have a point of allowed staffing before you can get paid for hired help. Find out what that number is and until you get there, be willing to use interns and other professional help that will allow you to be in touch, out in front, always networking, and the face of your sales engine. Top sales guys are face-to-face with their clients more than not. They get the importance of making the relationship and that emotional connection breeds referrals. Desk jockeys do not get this. They are typically hiding behind their phones and do not like the face-to-face. This alone, can be the difference in you advancing your sales.

Successful people evolve. Strive to be the better you. Accept every invite for free education that increases your sales skills set. Do not believe you know everything and do not sit back on the laurels of what made you successful because it is sure to change. I recall, after winning three to four years of annual sales contests in a later era of mortgage sales, being told to dust off my trophy case because this was a whole new market. They were right; what I did back in the day, I could no longer do, but I evolved through it, and still rose to the top to win. I was not a one hit wonder, and that, my friends, makes a career. It's about negotiating a series of wins through ever changing markets and a willingness to move with the needle. Make no mistake; some tried-and-true traits will always be true.

Be hard working and working smart. I believe the things above will make you a better sales guy. End of discussion.

"You don't need a Fan Club to achieve your goals, create your own momentum."

~ PixelPaperHearts.com

CHAPTER 20

Finding Gold!

THE ART OF FINDING CONSISTENT TOP SALES

EVER FEEL LIKE A GERBIL ON A WHEEL? You're running hard every day but feel like you're getting nowhere? Well, look around you.

One thing is certain—sales people who are finding the gold will continue to do it consistently. Also, when they strike it rich, you can bet on them running the gold mine dry before moving on to the next one.

So, this then begs the question, HOW are some sales people inherently unable to find gold AT ALL?? The answers are simple; they aren't looking in the right place.

TOP 3 REASONS SUCCESSFUL SALES PEOPLE STRIKE GOLD!

Focus Daily on Profit and Money-Making Tasks.

Top Sales People innately know that their next three paychecks are coming from today's ability to stay in the prospecting pocket. Top Sales people will service their clients well, manage their pipelines efficiently, and they quickly return to marketing, prospecting, and networking to stay in that pocket 80% of their time. Less vigorous sales people sit on their three sales like they have laid the golden egg, obsess on the things they can't control, and become completely distracted daily with their to-do lists (which are by and far made up of non-money-making tasks).

Have a Great Map for Finding Gold (Sales).

Top Sales People go after the gold. They are not afraid to seek opportunities with high volume referral partners and clientele who will leverage their current sales into the next set of referrals.

I have consistently seen mediocre and poor sales people migrate to whoever wants to talk to them at networking events rather than stepping up to go for the guy or gal who is surrounded by dozens of wanting suitors.

Top Sales people believe they have something to offer, have a value proposition, and have a speech on deck for the moment they get the ear of that top producing referral partner. Top Sales people maximize opportunity, recognizing that if the decision maker's ear is available for only five minutes, they must be ready to leverage that five into ten and on to the next step, whether it's deepening the relationship or asking for the sale. They are mentally prepared for the No, not afraid to get the No several times before getting the YES, and they completely believe they will get the YES. An important distinction is they have done homework and researched their targets to know they aren't mining barren land.

Focus on Results.

Top Sales People focus on how much they need to fill the machine to maintain a consistent level of sales. They also know when to shift gears if they come to a dry well.

Mediocre sales people tend to believe they can change the outcome of a sale they made and will push forward in disbelief if the sale is not rendering results. They will keep going to the referral partner, who literally has nothing for them, with the idea that together they will grow into sales. While it's good to have growth partners, having nothing but this type of referral partner will bleed a sales person dry of resources while rendering little gold.

Top Sales people will minimize these fruitless relationships and go after the ones that render immediate sales, and continue to do so, on a consistent basis. They are always focused on the results of their actions and know that they must get results to raise their game. In short, they must get nuggets of gold while mining for the big find and will not get caught up panning for false gold and weeds in pursuit of the ideal.

I've had the pleasure of working with all kinds of sales people. It is my belief and my faith that I can grow any sales person into a top producer with lessons that teach how to work smart and focus on execution and measuring results consistently. I've seen many sales people advance to be their team's next best producer. I have handed over trophies to guys and gals who I know worked hard and fought hard for their results. It is exciting and rewarding to relate a great underdog story knowing that you played a part in helping make that success happen. Top Sales is a simple game of daily focus and consistent action.

Prospect for Results

My best advice for both sales people and leaders of sales people is, be clear about the distinction between activity and results. Mistaking these actions will plummet sales down a mine shaft that can take months to dig your way out.

Which is this scenario, Activity or Results:

> *You pack up the hiking gear, head out to the river, pan rocks for days and never find gold. You worked just as hard as, or harder than the guy who was fishing one stream over and knew where to go.*

And therein lies the difference.

He went where the gold was to be found and you did not. You both did just as much mining; but who did more prospecting? Who came away with results? Next time, shoulder your way into his square foot of mining space and find that nugget of gold. Think about that. It's a simple change of location and requires the same effort. Make the change!

"We do not fear the unknown. We fear what we think we know about the unknown."

~ Teal Swan

CHAPTER 21

Ask and You Shall Receive

VITAL SALES TIPS FOR THOSE AFRAID TO ASK DIRECTLY FOR A SALE!

WE ALL ENTERED THE SALES FIELD sideways. It's true. Nobody wrote, 'A Salesman!' on their Kindergarten paper when asked, "What do you want to be when you grow up?"

Somewhere as we matured to adulthood, a friend or family member introduced us to a job that was in sales, and suddenly we were thrust into the front line of a job that required customer interaction, product knowledge, service skills, and of course sales skills.

How did it happen for you? Did you soar right away because you inherently possessed some of the basic people skills so highly treasured in sales? That was true for me as I genuinely love talking to people, and I am good at learning my product. Did you attempt to master an awkward script by over analyzing the proper way to speak to people while rattling off benefits of the product, and not in the smoothest way? That is closer to the experience most novices in sales relate.

We all know sales guys who should not be in sales. We have all had that guy or gal we had to have the talk with and explain that they were not cut out for sales. I also will say that top sales people often simply out-work their competition; I've seen this as often as I've seen the skilled sales person succeed.

What is it that separates successful sales people, no matter how they came to the craft or why they choose to stay, from those who are not successful? -Failure to ask for the business.

Even the most talented and experienced sales guys must practice, 'the ask.' This is the number one reason that top sales people excel. They are not afraid to point blank ask for the business, or they have mastered the technique of overcoming their fears of rejection. Either way, they ask, and they get business far more often than do the guys who just shows up. Think back to the gold mining analogy. When you step into the stream that has nuggets of gold sparkling through the running water, you will fail to get that gold if you do not dip your pan into the water and scoop up the nuggets. Ask or the gold will go to the next person.

This lesson hit home for me during one of my first District sales management jobs, over a decade and a half ago. I had a mystery to solve. There were 80 sales guys in a call center with eight sales managers. All of their phones rang off the hooks; all the team punched the same clock, put in the same hours, made the same quantity of calls. Why did some get twice the sales? I solved the mystery by listening to recorded sales calls. I learned the best techniques. The guys and gals hitting the high sales numbers had 'the ask' down pat. They asked the person on the other end of the line for referrals. They Knew when to pull the trigger and didn't over sell or under sell. And more, it was an eye-opening lesson for me and one I've never forgotten.

TIPS TO ASK FOR THE BUSINESS EVERY TIME!

Show Up Prepared and Do Not Leave Empty Handed

Great sales people do not go home empty handed. They also know that showing up with donuts and pizza, making small talk for several hours a day, and handing out marketing flyers is not enough. I have seen many a guy or gal show up and spend hours at their referral accounts, then walk away empty handed, WHILE watching their competition walk in and out with sales.

The difference often is in asking. Yes. You must ask for the sale. But long before then, you must look at your prospects and ask,

"Who has something for me today?"

"Who has questions about this program?"

"Who has a lead for me?"

The answers to these questions will take you a long way toward being the sales person walking out of the door with the sale instead of the eternal visitor waiting in the lobby with a box of stale donuts.

The Door Is Never Permanently Shut

Learn to recognize the difference between No and Not Now. And more importantly, get over your fear of No. In truth, No is always Not Now, unless you never come back. As sales people, we continue to work accounts; we go back to the same well often. People will warm up to you and come to expect your direct sales style. If you are consistently connecting with them at the same time each week, and you ask every time for business, they will begin to have business for you. Try it!

Top Sales People Never Forget

Top Sales people never forget to ask. They never forget. I have been surveying my top producers for years. So many times, the simple best tip they will give is that they ask for the business. When I first saw this comment in surveys, I thought it was too simple to be true, but it proved, over and over again, to be the missing ingredient that catapults a hard-working sales person to success.

Also, remember your competition is asking. It's like going to a dance. You're standing in the outside circle wanting to get in the mix. Do you ask for a dance? Or do you stand against the wall, watching while other people dance with your date? It's your choice. Decide to ask; Or not.

If you chose sales, get comfortable and good at asking; otherwise, hang up the brief case for another line of work that is less taxing, less satisfying, and most likely less financially rewarding.

Oh, and by the way. Top sales people never forget to ask.

Come from a Genuine Place

In asking for business, believe in why you are the best choice for your customer or client. If you believe you are better, or have more to offer, if you are confident and do an excellent job, then you will be asking with the idea that you are going to give a better service to the person than the next guy; so in this way, you can think of yourself as a hero. Top Sales people believe in this. They are cut throat about their confidence; and truthfully, they simply step up to the plate and swing way more often than the next guy, and thus their batting average is far better.

I am so proud to be a sales person, to help folks with the American dream of home ownership. I honed my sales skills for decades, and then I started teaching the tips that helped me win sales contests. I've earned a client base that is now three decades strong, and I've helped grow hundreds of sales people into the next best sales guy or gal. It's rewarding. I'm not afraid to ask. I ask often and I'm not afraid of being told, not now.

The real question is, Are you asking? Think about it. It may truly be that one simple change is all it takes to get yourself to the next level.

The Mindset

HOW MUCH POWER DOES THE MIND HAVE to change our physical course in our jobs, in our lives, and our worlds? The truth is 100% of it. I have put together many seminars and classes that one might label philosophical or mentally minded. (Or just mental. Ha!) In those events and in the chapters that follow, I outline traits that we use to control our minds and discuss various mental aspects that pull us from the path we've chosen. The ability to control our mind is real, not a theory: tested and true.

These chapters are the culmination of my experience, writings I've read, and applicable traits observed in successful people who, by the power of their minds, drive to a success that is superior to those who believe their minds are on auto pilot and that they aren't really in control.

You drive yourself, even when you don't realize it, until you've driven off the road, or worse, have an event occur that results in assessing your life.

Life happens; and how we react to life's heartaches and disappointment and to work stresses and fires, is a testament and the reality of the person you can become after reading this very vital section. I know, because I have had to crawl out of some pretty deep holes. I cherish the years I put together where I soared, but I walk the earth with the knowledge that if I feel great today, it is a gift.

Humans are fragile, and we break down. I don't hold myself to a crazy perfect standard, nor do I expect that of my students.

"I don't know when I will stop climbing. I am not sure any-one ever does. I think as people we pause at times to check out the view, sit back, and reflect on how far we've come. For me, climbing is what keeps me alive. Knowing there is more to see, conquer, and experience keeps me moving forward."

~ C.B.

CHAPTER 22

Analysis Paralysis?

ARE YOU YOUR BIGGEST OBSTACLE?

WE ALL KNOW PEOPLE WHO SHARE their big plans at the weekly sales meeting, and then the next week, share their plans, and the next week share their plans, and the next week share their plans...getting the point?

Yeah, there is such a thing as over planning, over analyzing and simply put, plain old over-thinking.

What separates the guy who acts, who takes the difficult first step, from those people who remain at the starting line, mapping out their course? The answer may surprise you. It is FEAR. Fear is what keeps people from moving.

It may not even be apparent to the person who is stuck because, in their minds, they are pragmatic risk takers. They look at their plan from all sides. They vehemently defend choice to avoid action until they have all the answers. They ask endless questions and digest the answers and then think of more questions. Meanwhile, the clock ticks and they fail to enter the race. Others have completed the course and are already in the winner's circle collecting their medals.

Are you the person who over thinks? If so, or if you manage people like this, there are simple actions you can take, traits you can learn to recognize, to encourage change that will enable the first crucial steps towards action and success.

Prescribe a Solution for Likely Obstacles

Consider the obstacles and determine the worst-case scenario. Then quickly write down the solution or prescription for the problem and move on. I would write no more than three legitimate obstacles because people with analysis paralysis will write down dozens of probable and unlikely issues so that they feel satisfied they have thought of every imaginable problem.

The truth is, successful people don't need all the answers, they can think and react on the fly, and as such, know there are out of scope issues likely to affect their plans. To move past this, if you are super analytical, write your 'out of scope' obstacles on a separate paper. Understand there is no remedy at the onset of this plan for those obstacles; that you will be left to think in the moment if they occur.

Write down the FIRST STEP in your plan

If it's a new sales plan for the next year, your first step might be Organize Office or Analyze Referral Network List. Then put a date to start next to it, put it in all applicable calendars. You have now picked a start time and you MUST start on that day.

Timeline Action Steps

To keep the plan in motion, write down the next three steps and timeline them. If you are managing this, be sure to schedule and perform check-ins as your sales person takes these crucial steps to get moving. If they (or you) are stuck, ask a peer to help you get started.

All the planning in the world will not prepare you completely for action. Fear is a debilitating thing. It keeps people from reaching their dreams. Sometimes we all like the safe little place we are in. Yet look at how success is depicted and perceived. In every remarkable success story, movie, or book, success comes to the one who innately acts easily, who is not afraid of risking it and losing it or failing in the process of tweaking a plan to success. You can't win anything sitting still and over thinking the outcome.

I am a planner and a teacher of business planning. And I am the first to admit, that for those in analysis paralysis, the plan is not the issue. It is often literally the taking of the first step that has to happen. Keep this in mind, like a ball rolling down hill; if you need the nudge at the top (and you know who YOU are!) then make sure you have someone poised in a position to shove. -Gently at first and firmly as needed.

I see this failure to step out more predominantly with inexperienced sales people, and I get it. They want to make sure they have all their ducks in a row; they fear being discovered as someone who doesn't have all the answers. I would argue, nobody has all the answers, and in an ever-changing world, all sales people must self-educate. In reality, the new person may be more prepared than veteran sales people who have not advanced or evolved with the times. It's simple. Stop over-thinking it. Period. As Yoda says, *Do or do not. There is no try.*

In the end, paralysis is about self-confidence. I have seen sales guys who would gripe about the quality of spoon fed, scrubbed leads, and then conversely, I would see guys who could soar with a phone book and a telephone. They would find the deal, the opportunity and close it. The difference in these two types of people is someone with confidence and someone who lacks it.

Get off the sideline, jump in the race. If you're afraid of this, then please park your car, and pick a different line of work.

Seriously.

"Quiet the mind and The Soul will speak."

~ Ma Jaya Sati Bhagavati

CHAPTER 23

Motivation Mining

DAILY STEPS FOR SELF-IMPROVEMENT

LITERALLY MY FAVORITE PASTIME! When I get asked what I do for fun, I wish I could admit that I spend hours upon hours searching sites for motivational quotes or writings that I read and feel inspired by; what does that make me? Strange? Normal? Smart?

I believe I live in a perpetual state of astonishment at the human ability to redefine itself through applicable, positive change. I am a living science project that has proven that 100% of my applied positive changes render better results than my prior dismal state. It's a no brainer. I can't understand why more people do not know that the secret to their poverty, their weakness, their addiction, their depression is changeable (albeit difficult) through daily steps of self-improvement. There is always more you can do to affect positive change.

Ever ask yourself what your personal obligation is for feeding your own motivation? Ever come to realize we can control our thoughts? That we do not have to be a passenger in the car of our mind, but the driver?

How does this work? It's simple. We feed our minds daily with many things. I have listed below what I believe to be the top *Mind feeders* in basic daily interaction:

- *People* we are around and who we have chosen to be in our lives

- *Atmosphere*: Are your surroundings happy?

- *Voyeurism*: Do you migrate to dark articles, news, depressing stories and programs on TV? And if you do, ever thought about choosing lighter materials? Motivating material? How about Sports? This could be a game changer because the motivators that sports bring out in us: hope, spirit, competition, patriotism, anticipation, pride, and more, are keys to success in almost every endeavor.

- *Readership*: What do you read? When you pick up a book, is the content motivational? It's ok to choose mind escape material. I often do this when traveling; pick up the serial magazines to give my aching brain a break from all I feed its constant, never-ending engine. When I really want to feed my mind, I buy a motivational story, and I watch motivational movies.

- *Water Cooler Club*: Be aware of who you hang with. Are you with positive people at work? Do you migrate to the commissary club? Know that YOU can change any club you are in simply by being the example.

- *Introspection*: How much empathy do you show? Are you quiet and introspective? This is one trait I find to be a real deal killer in my personal relationships. I have a truly hard time relating to people who do not have the ability to listen and then think for themselves. Please do not preach to me about your problems without presenting the other side. I guess my perspective is carved out of three decades of leadership although I've seen plenty of so called leaders who lack it.

Motivation has to start with you recognizing how you are feeding yourself, positioning yourself, navigating yourself in this world. Do you steer towards troubled waters? Are you a magnet for drama? An honest look in the mirror will tell you.

Only you can adjust your path by looking inward. Many of us lack the ability to motivate by self-searching. True growth comes from this, by admitting to ourselves our weaknesses, tendencies, and adversities, especially those that are self-afflicted.

The heart of your personal motivation-What is it?

We are all wired differently. We are all drawn to different things although we may have similarities. What is your motivation? What inspires you and gets you hustling? What is your heart's desire?

I asked myself this question somewhere in my first decade in the banking business. I had not aspired to be a banker. My inspiration is writing and teaching, and I desired, from the time I was a young girl, to be in the medical field, with a specialty in sports medicine athletics. I had my aerobic instructing license early on and used that knowledge, as well as my nutrition certification, to teach health and physical wellness. This background has served me well in my personal health and wellness, of course, but Math is a far distance from aerobics.

How did I end up in banking? Well, I guess by chance. I got my first job in banking as a teller. What started as a way to pay the bills, has become a passion within which I have advanced over and over again spanning more than three decades.

I have been lucky, truly, to be gifted with a few wonderful traits, such as hard work, competitiveness, an ability to adapt, to advance, and to inspire. It was never my desire to lend money to people. There is great honor in lending; it's simply that my desire is to teach, specifically, to teach others what I know in life, what I have learned through hard times and success.

My inspiration comes when I sit before a typewriter (or keyboard) and put my thoughts into words. It is always my hope to inspire others, help them advance past a mental block, to teach a new skill or simply to philosophically evoke a catalyst in them to be better.

Much of my job as a senior leader in banking involves writing, teaching, and motivating. However, I can't lose sight of the primary purpose of my work, which is to increase the bottom line for my company through pointed sales instruction. I admit to taking every chance given to pepper in life lessons. I am full in my mind and heart when a student shares a heartfelt thank you. I teach from a genuine place in my desire to break through learning walls and increase the statistics of learning with powerful and meaningful words.

What is your heart's desire, inspiration, and motivation?

Take the time to learn the answer to this question, because your answer will lead you down a path in life of happiness, especially when you align that with a money-making job. You will prosper. You will find the tedious work invigorating, you will find the real meaning of helping others within it, and you will be taken care of through a motivation to perform.

If you simply are chasing the dollar, you see the earnings abilities but hate what you do, I strongly urge you to reconsider your profession. I mean that sincerely. We are here in life to be happy. Life is short. You must find your middle ground.

"When there is no enemy within, the enemies outside cannot hurt you."

~ African proverb

CHAPTER 24

The Enemy Within

FIVE INTERNAL TRAITS THAT DERAIL SUCCESS

EVER FIND YOURSELF SCRATCHING your head at the guy or gal in the office who clearly doesn't realize they are sabotaging their own success?

No? Well then, you may want to take a hard look in the mirror, because every office has one, make sure it's not YOU!

There are many personality traits that I consider devastating to being or managing successful sales people. I find that there are five that are the most prevalent. Are any of these self-sabotaging traits derailing your success and the success of those who you lead?

Self-Doubt

We all need to bounce ideas off each other and collaborate. Viewing a situation through the eyes and perceptions of many perspectives ensures a thorough consideration of potential obstacles and outcomes. The person who asks opinions and shares ideas, but then never executes is plagued with self-doubt. It happens to everybody at some point. For those under pressure to deliver results, fear can be especially limiting.

There is a solution. Pragmatic Risk Assessment (PRA) is a practice that even the most timid people can regularly exercise to get past fears. The technique involves assessing your pros and cons, and then eliminate the cons, one by one, by applying a solution. Then change to focus on the Pros and how to achieve success. People who are riddled with fear need to reason their perception of risk; fear limits the ability to act but many don't realize it.

If this is how you operate, I strongly suggest you get a journal. Write your projects, goals, and plans down on paper. Then, regularly go through a PRA exercise to get (and stay!) mentally unblocked. Make this a habit. You will find yourself acting far more often. Bonus tip: timeline your own results. In other words, give yourself an expected date to take the first steps on your plan that will allow you to get past step one; the rest should flow.

Over-Complicator

Over complication is in the Analysis Paralysis wheelhouse as we've already discussed. This trait is less about being stuck in the analysis stage, and more about having so many plans and so many intricate details of a plan that it's difficult to know where to start.

This is also the plague of people who are afraid to get started, who are unsure of themselves, and who keep searching for answers. Typically, over complicators will apply systems and plans, layer after layer, and never really do anything with great conviction. These people confuse and complicate even the simplest of things.

If you see yourself in this, strip everything back to the bone. Go to the base of your plan and rebuild. Master one step before taking the next. Plans are to be completed and contests won, one day and one step at a time. It's really that simple. If you are managing someone who over-complicates things, guide them to follow the same strip-down process.

Be aware, that if you happen to combine the trait of impatience with over complication, you tend to revise plans too soon, before allowing enough time for the first plan to play out. Be the guy or gal who shifts gears when needed and does not shift before you should.

You Allow Distractions to Distract

I call this the Butterfly Affect. You spend so much time discovering the world around you that you are unable to look at your own problems, plans, and necessary steps and tactics. You are easily distracted, social to a point of fault, and you value interaction and conversation more than self-work and results.

If this is not you but you work with someone like this, you may dread seeing them in the office, as they may be distracting you from getting your work done.

If you don't know anyone like that and as you are reading this, you are standing in the center of your office, on your mobile, leaning on the cubicle of the guy or gal next to you, YOU may be the person distracting others. Sit down, shut up, and focus on money making tasks. Period.

Be aware that the internet is a huge trap for you. Think of the butterfly or moth circling closer and closer to the insect zapper until finally, so caught up, that escape is impossible. When you use the internet for work, take care to not end up 10 sites sideways.

Same caution about making personal calls at work. You are so social that keeping the subjects of your phone calls, in the work zone is a challenge; and when you fail to manage that challenge, the butterfly in you totally derails your entire day, week, or month.

This is literally one of the top detractors of an entire office success. Hiring too many butterflies will affect how everyone functions, and you will dish out a lot of money for social hours as your efficiency and conversion rates plummet.

Act Like Switzerland!

It's easy to repeat fun gossip. Does no harm, right? If it's already common knowledge, how does it hurt to repeat private matters and share in the office gossip? In the same process, it's easy to gossip about customers or get sucked into a customer service dispute. It seems natural to take the side of your co-worker over that of an ignorant customer and go on the defense when a person is blatantly wrong or inept. Right?

No. Not the best practice in either situation. Any of us can throw down or sink to immature levels of arbitration or debate. Resist. Staying classy is necessary even if it's hard to do.

Diplomacy is a trait that great leaders possess. The ability to say something difficult or settle an office dispute between two people without causing more grief in the process, keeping confidential information, and really being willing to take a leadership role are great traits for any team member to claim.

To be strong in the face of significant adversity, be the person who always shows diplomacy. Do so even in the little things; it is much better than being labeled the office gossip. When you can be this person, you are already winning.

Will you fail at this at times? Likely so. The key is to practice all the time. When adversity rises in your area, for any reason, whether with a co-worker or a customer, you will be ready. Be the example of great service, educate the ignorant, and tolerate the inept. Do not hurt yourself, your relationships, and your success by being the guy who thinks he won the debate. Customer service debates have no winners.

Absent, Even when Present

One of the worst things I see professionals do is give less than 100% of their focus to a class, meeting, one on one, or even with customer appointments. Whoever you are meeting with, give them 100% of your attention. Put aside your phone, hang your out of office flag, set an auto reply on your texts and emails. Simply state that you are in a meeting and will return calls, emails, and texts at X time.

We live in a time of electronic distraction. It is no longer meme worthy to see six people sitting at a restaurant table all looking at their iPhone. Just because we constantly receive information doesn't mean we need to answer in real time.

The real challenge for those inclined to being easily distracted is that electronics make us available 24/7. We used to have delays. Emails came in after hours, and we didn't see them until the next day. Friends and family called us after work or left messages on our home answering machines that we could return when we wanted. Now, every bit of personal and business communication flows to us in real time, wherever we are. It is too easy to be constantly watching our electronic devices.

What is the solution? Be present, in the moment. Stop multitasking and sneaking looks at notifications when the meeting is virtual. Get out of the habit of being a real time texter, emailer, and caller. Get back to LIVING in your client's moment, your friend's moment, your spouses and children's moments, and more than anything, living in a fashion that allows you to be productive. iPhone could single handedly have stripped the entire universal work force of 40% of its work focused hours, if not greater. Think about it.

"Your body can stand almost anything. It's your mind that you have to convince."

~ HPLYRIKZ.com

CHAPTER 25

Controlling Stress and Freeing Your Mind

PROFESSIONAL AND PERSONAL OR-GANIZATION

FOR THE BEST PART OF THE PAST TWO decades I have been a senior sales executive, a business owner, a fundraiser, and a health enthusiast.

I work in a high demand, fast paced, all stakes deadline environment, driven on constantly assessed metrics and results—

all while managing a home, traveling for work, raising a child, and trying to be a healthy professional.

Do you ever feel as if you are chasing your own nonexistent tail? That was me for many years, especially early in my career. My life changed when I mastered the art of compartmentalizing.

I would love to say that I did this through personal insight, but the truth is, I did this through professional training. Training that taught me how to off-board the clutter and chaos and make organization out of all of it. Training that taught me how to shut off the work brain and turn on the home brain, in a flip of a switch. Training and experience that allowed me to synthesize it all into a simple system.

Once I learned the *Ten Tips for Professional and Personal Organization*, my life changed. I knew that I was in complete control and that living in balance was possible.

I teach these tips to professionals who are equally hectic in their own busy lives, and it is one of the most raved about classes I teach. I hope it helps you as well.

Get it Out of Your Head and Onto Paper

Do you know that everything you need to do is swirling around in your head? Do you know that your brain (or as I like to call it, your human computer) will keep sending you memory messages to remind you that these things must be done? What is that chaos doing to your stress levels? -To the output of magnificent work results? What is the price you are paying for this level of overwhelming thinking?

Consider how often a random task pops into you head when you are busy doing something important. These memory messages are like getting social media notifications on your computer: important to remember and know about and also easy to shut down. The simple act of writing things down will off-board or shut down the reminder; almost like clicking *Dismiss* on your computer to stop the pop-up reminders.

Using a working journal is a straightforward way to clean up all your repetitive thoughts and leave your mind clear. When you do this, your level of creativity, your ability to think, ability to digest reading, to absorb meeting materials, and even clearly learn class education is at a far higher and more receptive level than you would be left with otherwise, with all that chaos happening in your brain.

Using the working journal daily can physically change your entire outlook on the quality and happiness of your work and your personal life. You can be a more attentive partner and spouse, parent and coach. Simply put, organizing thoughts and off-boarding these thoughts can lead to a healthier life style, one you control and one that gets amazing results.

Buy A Journal. It may be a blank journal, or you might get a Day Timer with single full pages to represent each day, like this:

#1. Top Line: Day and Date on each page

#2. Second Line: Your list of Professional To Do's

Each to do item should then be labeled either A or B. A for Absolutely Must Be Done Today and B for Secondary Task, does not need to be done today.

#3. Third Line: Personal to do items.

Only list tasks here that you MUST do today. All other personal to do items can be listed on the appropriate page, so if you know you need to drop off dry cleaning on Wednesday, write it in the personal to do item on Wednesday. Simple.

#4. Fourth Line: Due from others.

Every time you give someone something to do that is owed back to you, you will write it here. You will give it an owner's name and a due date with a description of the thing due.

Example: Due Friday - Sue - Accounting for September.

#5. Fifth Line: Projects

List all projects needing to be done this week that aren't single to do items. These things may take several hours to complete or several days. You should apply an expected timeline to these. These should be bigger items that need more attention and MUST be done that week.

Example: Create the Excel Spreadsheet for the new coaching platform-2 hours.

#6. When to do your journal?

The last thing you are going to do every night is write tomorrows' Management Journal Page. You will do several things in reviewing your day and as your day has transpired.

First. You will put a strike though the To Do Items completed. You will strike out those things collected that were due from others as complete as well.

Second. You will circle all things not completed; carry those over to the next day. Apply an A and B to each item again. Please note, if you carry an A item over more than twice, you aren't prioritizing correctly.

Finally. Your new list should be neat, clean, each section filled as outlined above, so when you wake up and begin working the next day, you are able to open your journal and work with it at your side. As things transpire though out the day, you can write to do items into proper days based on due dates and time needed to complete.

#7. Learn to say NO today to things that you can't fit in your schedule.

We all accept too much work; the word NO is not pleasing to say, so we avoid it. Instead say, *I can do this for you by tomorrow*. That's not a NO, and it gives you a whole extra day.

When you begin to use this Management Journal System, you will discover you know much better if you can handle taking a job on today or tomorrow. You may even see that you are booked out days ahead.

#8. Journal versus Electronic Calendar.

Your electronic calendar should reflect physical appointments for calls and meetings and have time blocked to work on the to do list. Some days I have 3 two-hour blocks to handle my work load and project list, leaving only two more hours for meetings.

#9. Bulk like activities into a single day.

For time management sake, book your physical appointments all in one day, morning, noon, and night if need be. These will allow for to do tasks and project work on the opposing days. Since these days work from home or casual days in an office are not unusual practices, bulking your meeting time may also allow you to be dressed professionally and accordingly for face-to-face meetings, and conversely, be able to relax and be comfortable while working your project and to do lists.

#10. Walk Away.

Have a timeline on work ending. Create a schedule that fits your workload and best practices AND that allows you to walk away entirely. Perhaps this means working late some nights or getting up extra early other days.

Whenever that ending time comes, you, at that time, walk away from your work, your phone, your desk, your email, and you live in the space of your family, your home, your life, and your personal world.

You must do this. I realize that is easy to say. I have worked all my adult life needing to provide weekend and often evening services. How do you achieve this balance? How do you walk away when you know there's more to be done?

I have learned that the same people who called me at night and weekends were willing, when asked, to speak to me during business hours, on lunch breaks, and early evening. If I had to accommodate weekend work, I would put it all into a Saturday time frame of 2-3 hours, and I would let my family know I had to work.

This seems like such a straightforward process, too simple, stupidly simple. But, these eight steps are harder than you think. Difficult and vitally important. Create these organizational habits in your life.

Most people work from a to do list even if that list is in their head. Does yours have everything and the kitchen sink listed? Are the tasks prioritized? Have you separated personal tasks from professional to dos? Have you organized in a manner that allows you to be present in whatever world you are living in with your brain free of all that clutter? Incorporate these ten steps into your life. You will feel more productive and in truth, be more productive and able to enjoy more both the professional and personal sides of your life.

Good luck. Feel free to ask me questions! I have hundreds of people who use this system and tell me it has lifted the weight of stress and organization to new levels never experienced.

"Your energy introduces you before you even speak."

~ The Vibrant Mind

CHAPTER 26

Reticular Activator System

ACTIVATE THE SUPER SALESMAN WITHIN YOU

I KNOW EXACTLY WHERE I WAS WHEN I first learned about Reticular Activation. I was on the sales floor of one of my old company's district offices in Tampa, Florida, listening to a peer Sales Manager share his understanding of how this worked. He was impressive and articulate. He used examples and practical application so that his audience could apply his lesson easily.

It changed my life in sales. I have been paying forward this lesson for nearly 15 years now. It can and will change your sales results immediately.

The definition of Reticular Activation is this: The ascending reticular activating system (ARAS), also known as the extra thalamic control modulatory system, or simply the reticular activating system (RAS), is a set of connected nuclei found in the brains of vertebrates. The RAS is responsible for regulating wakefulness and sleep-wake transitions.

RAS has many functions. One of them is filtering. Just as a secretary controls who visits an executive's office, RAS acts as a filter to your brain. Our conscious mind can take in far less data than your subconscious mind. Our conscious intake is billions per parts of data less than we absorb subconsciously. This huge difference is relevant because, once you understand how this works, all that subconscious processing power becomes a boost you can use.

Here's an example. When you bought your last car, it's likely that you researched that car, test drove that car, shopped for that car. Did you notice that suddenly, you saw this car on the road at a far higher frequency? The reason is your RAS filtered what your conscious mind noticed and allowed your brain to pull that focus to the top. There were NOT more cars of this kind around you than before. You simply told your brain this car was of interest, and your RAS set out to bring those cars into focus, to the Top of Mind.

A second example might be when you hear a strange word you've never heard before, BUT then you hear it again and again. Is that just a coincidence? No. It's your RAS at work. Your filter is bringing it forward.

What about a song you like, that you are playing often and suddenly, it seems to be playing everywhere. RAS again at work.

Now that you understand what RAS is and how it works to filter things, let's put this to work in a money-making way. Let's bring sales Top of Mind. When you get up in the morning and you begin your routine, what do you think about?

What if you choose to think about all the sales you are going to make that day? What if, when you dress, part of your routine is to put 12 business cards in your pocket, with the belief that you will hand them to 12 new people a day and to share what you do?

What are the opportunities within a day to find 12 people who you believe would want to help you make a sale?

What if I told you to put 25 business cards in your pocket per day; and that for every person you gave one to, you also handed them a second or even third card and say, "I build my business on referrals and would appreciate your help to share that I do X for a living?"

Would these people want to help you? (TIP: Use human words when selling. People innately want to HELP people.)

Still not sure who would help you? Let's name people in your inner sphere of influence who you might hand a card to every day, starting with when you leave your driveway on your way to work:

- Convenience store attendant where you stop for gas and gum
- Clerks at the coffee shop
- Teachers and other parents at your child's school
- Your mechanic and coworkers.
- Your landscaper and coworkers.
- Your hairdresser and coworkers.

- Your child's sports coach and all his peers.

- Your handy man.

- Your postal clerk or delivery person.

- All the neighbors on your street.

- All the people in the businesses on your street.

- All the people in the businesses at your place of employment in your building and on your business street.

- All your friends and their friends and families.

- Your family.

- Your parent's friends.

- Your veterinarian and all their coworkers.

- Your doctor or dentist and coworkers.

- Your child's pediatrician and all their coworkers.

- Any medical providers and coworkers.

- Your spa and all their employees.

THE LIST IS ENDLESS!!!!

My final question is deceptively simple and yet is truly the key to applying this system.

Is Sales at The Top of Your Mind every day?

When you realize that sales are all around you and that people you give business to and interact with want to help you, then you will have it come to your mind constantly. It's up to YOU to feed your subconscious. We SEE what we want; it's the basic Law of Attraction and in truth, the Law of Attraction can't work without RAS and RAS can't work until you feed it what you want. It's really that simple.

Bonus Tip (Using Mortgage Sales as an example, but is applicable to any type of product sales): What do you think is at Top of Mind for your clients who are buying, selling, or refinancing a home?

Their RAS keeps them aware of people around them at work, neighbors, family members, and friends who are buying, selling, and refinancing a home. Thus, your greatest place to gain referrals is the current customer you are working with. THEY have referrals. THEY know who around them is doing what they are doing right now, AND you are displaying your impeccable knowledge and service right now so asking them to refer you should be simple.

Sales is not hard, but it is not for the lazy. If you are smart and you have any kind of work ethic, there is an endless supply of money waiting for you!

"Have faith, hold on, stay strong. Believe in who you are. You can change anything you want to in your life. You have the power to change your thoughts, your situation in-to a better one. Make it happen. Live life to the fullest and never take anything or anyone for granted. Life is fragile treat it as a gift and thank God for all you have."

~ Unknown

CHAPTER 27

Closing Thoughts

A WORK IN PROGRESS

I AM NOT SURE AT WHAT AGE or point in a person's life one says, I'm done! I am hanging up my hat and calling it a day. I am moving on to the next thing, professionally speaking.

I just know that I thought by now I would be saying that. Instead, I am still growing, still climbing, and still searching for more peace, spreading more love, more education, and I have a lot more to do to be satisfied.

I will admit, I think of my end game more often in recent years. I have few regrets but some incredibly difficult things I have overcome, and for that, I am stronger, am prouder, and probably a little more callused than the guy whose dreams fell in his lap. I have come to realize people want leaders.

When I was afraid to speak publicly for so many years, it came to me that humans want a voice and a vision to follow; that most people desire a strong direction from someone willing to take the lead.

I was born to lead. Even though I've had moments when I resented the weight of leadership, for the most part, I am comfortable in that role. Even more so, I enjoy who and where I am now: witnessing my own self-development, and teaching and coaching others. The rewards seem closer, the respect seems greater, and the results seem more profound, on both sides.

I have discovered that as humans we desire happiness, but we often look outward for those results. We are great at denying our own mistakes, impatient for change that benefits us, and lazy at the tasks required to make personal moves that are painful but necessary. We are ultimately dumb about our power. We must learn to control how we think, how we interact in our relationships, and how we navigate the world towards our dreams.

With this in mind, I have discovered a truth through personal losses, struggles, and disasters—all is doable, but we must reach our own breaking points to take the first step.

People will happily be unhappy for a very long time. When we begin our evolution from the dark places life can place us, the journey out of the dark and into that light, in any facet, is glorious and worthy of celebration.

The trick is staying in that place of multifaceted light. Evil and darkness creeps in sideways most of our lives. One wrong decision, one wrong move left or right, and suddenly, we are invisibly spiraling into a place we have no idea how difficult or impossible it will be to climb out of until we hit that bottom.

My life's goals are to help people make those changes; to help lift people up, save their careers, their lives, and to reach new goals and experience greater heights. I want to enlighten the human spirit, to demonstrate its limitless abilities through what I have personally experienced in my own struggles, from initial poverty to the health and career aspects from which I have risen.

While I do not preach to others, I am a person of faith; a fact that has likely seeped into the words throughout the pages of this book. I believe that when I have hit rock bottom in my life, it was God who lifted me up and showed me a path and helped me take the first difficult step towards the light.

I could not see that light sometimes. I am brutally aware of how a person's soul can die in the right or wrong circumstances and how hopeless it can feel when reaching around in the dark to overcome the impossible and find the staircase leading up.

Life is a series of highs and lows that all people experience. Yet, not all people experience those highs and lows in the same way. Think about it. How is it that some keep themselves in safe places, really living and facing the good and bad of taking risk, while others live safe, indifferent, benign lives that are satisfying but not fulfilling?

I consider myself a mental trainer. Much like a physical trainer, my job is to make a person think harder than they came to think, to work harder than they came to work, to work smarter than they currently are, and to see the goal line, get to the goal line, and celebrate their victories. The lessons of my life allow me to give guidance through dark times that lifts up and gives hope, direction, and consolation. Most of all sharing my own experience and the understanding that comes from knowledge allows them to fall and know they are not alone.

Everyone is capable of personal and professional greatness; yet I have seen people die from lack of mental strength. In truth it is the division of strong and weak. I have been both at various times in my life, fought through the dark and weakness, and prevailed—stronger in every way.

When I am winning, I thank God every day. When I am failing, I go to my knees asking him to help me find the light.

I have come to learn that my greatest strengths are also my greatest weaknesses, like seeing good in all people.

Pro: I can draw on the positive of any person.

Con: I can be blinded by their good side and ignore their bad side, I am generous.

Pro: I am giving.

Con: I am taken advantage of.

Pro: I am a positive person, I like sharing positive and emotional evoking quotes and stories that ignite emotion in my students.

Con: Evoking emotion annoys people who are emotionally disconnected; they can't relate and chastise these activities as senseless.

I have fought the battles of emotional strife and won. As I put the finishing touches on a 12-year book, written in pieces across the decade, I do so having suffered emotional setbacks.

I have battled mental illness, clinical depression that required treatment. Facing that was hard, and I chose to remain private, seeking the treatment in a confidential manner.

There were many months during which it was difficult to rise and work and give my ultimate focus with an expectation of impressive results. However, it was my job, and I refused to fail the people who depended on me.

One personal triumph came when, after a 32-year addiction to cigarettes, I decided one day to stop, cold turkey. I took a leap of faith, knowing I would go through the physical pain of addiction, the pangs of cravings, to get to the other side. Truthfully, I had been moving towards quitting for years, not liking it anymore, finding it stupid, inconvenient, and unattractive. Even so, I count this as a huge success and evidence that mind over matter does work.

I have faced illnesses and viruses that have been scary. Some of those times I had to physically crawl out of the place I was. I have faced the emotional mountain of being diagnosed with cancers. This news is paralyzing at first, both mentally and physically. And then, too soon to truly process how different life suddenly is, comes the painful, singular path of taking the treatment and praying that cancer would not come back stronger or spread.

I had to face hair loss this past year due to the treatments I received, all while remaining in the public eye as a female professional. I chose to accept this and all my health issues completely privately, without making a public statement, without looking for sympathy, or even empathy. Simply face it. Show up for the medical appointments. Go to work. Rinse and repeat until I am told I am ok.

I do not want to minimize this. I've faced cancer three times in three different ways and only a handful of people have been aware of this. During those times, every day felt like an eternity. I hid my pain, went early to bed, made a conscious choice to change diet, exercise, and wellness.

Each day included both physical and mental struggles until I could defeat my issue and move past it. That determination is what carried me through when I wanted to quit. It was commitment to and passion for my work that made me rise each day and take another step forward. Thankfully people depended on me to help guide them at work, so I chose to be a happy and inspirational coach while I privately suffered; facing this day by day, sometimes hour by hour, until I overcame those periods as well.

I will add, based upon my observation of many people around me, all human beings face some sort of mental illness at some point in their lives, whether permanent issues or onset issues; it is clear we are all in a battle to keep our sanity in check to varying degrees.

I am also convinced that active minds are why artists and geniuses go mad, because endless thoughts that wake you, that keep you awake, or keep you from sleeping are often not a conscious process but instead, brought on by an over-active brain over which we have little control. I have learned the methods to help myself, like writing in journals, and doing things I outlined in earlier chapters, that speak to mental compartmentalization.

I juggle an incredibly difficult schedule; travel, sometimes more than one city in one week, packing and unpacking, strange cities, often alone, lonely hotel rooms, quiet rental car drives, long hours, and separation from my family. I have balanced the phone on my shoulder, taking business calls while cooking dinner, taken mobile calls while juggling a child's schedule which, in and of itself, is a full-time job. I have had weeks tied to weeks where I didn't sit more than a solid hour to watch television and then would have to see a recorded program from weeks prior.

This life I live is not for everyone. My tireless schedule and work ethic comes from a place where I am super excited and happy with the life I chose and am living. I love what I do, love my life; I wake every day excited and happy that I am such a people person. I feel blessed even when I am tired. Completely blessed.

Every morning I wake and feel immediate elation and am eager to see what lies ahead in my day, excited to make a difference, happy to be living and thriving.

My goals have changed in life through this journey. I used to dream of being a famous motivational speaker. Now, I desire to reach whatever height God wants me to reach, to spread my positive word and if that height is national, international or whatever it is, I am up for the ride. Doing my best for as many people as I can is what matters to me, not doing it for notoriety.

It is interesting to note that, since I shifted this dream from personal notoriety to helping others with their gains, I have received far more accolades and rewards. I believe that is how God works. He must know you are coming from the right place before he rewards you.

One thing has remained true throughout my entire life— from that first run at the grade school political position to the current battle to remain relevant in a male dominated field as one of the top 2% of female senior leaders in the nation—and that is no matter how discouraging some years were with declining markets, company closure, corporate and industry consolidation, and personal difficulties, I woke every single morning ready to prove that I have a good heart, that I have what it takes to help others, to lead others, and to prevail against any obstacle no matter how high.

I can't see where my life is going because I choose to live in my moment, to live in the now. I know this past year was rewarding, that had this book been finished in the first year I started writing it, the words on these pages would not be as relevant as they are now, the lessons would not be as rich and meaningful; the reward of reaching this bucket list milestone would not be as grand. So, I believe this is happening as it should be, right now, after another decade of life has been survived, another decade of taking my profession through the most difficult of times ever in the history of mortgage finance.

I have come to be my own student in life, I do pause to reflect and learn and accept where I am. I am far more willing to realize the tough spot I may find myself in is only a step in a direction I believe is bringing me somewhere far greater, and I traded that thought process for a time when I thought the sad thing that was happening was the end of the world. We are resilient as human beings. We can write our comeback story, many times.

I hope in the end, this book has helped everyone who reads it. That someone finds a new skill, a new inspiration, a new way to look at an old problem or plague. I hope that it lifts people up, gives them faith and, moreover, makes everyone reading this know that anything they set their minds to is possible.

Anything!

ABOUT THE AUTHOR

CHRISTINE L. BECKWITH is the middle child of three girls in the Stiles family to younger sister Heidi Stiles and older sister, Tammy Trefrey. After growing up in Meredith NH, she left home at 18 to pursue her desire for a medical career attending college courses at Framingham State College in the fall of 1988. She ended up settling down in that area for over a decade. Christine pursued a banking career after taking a job on the teller line of a small credit union in Clinton MA and catching the bug for mortgage sales early in her career while assisting other loan officers as a processor.

Over the past three decades Christine has made her way through the ranks of originations as a Loan Officer, eventually a Branch Manager, Area Manager, District Manager, Regional Manager, and National Vice President to today her helm of a top ten medium financial sector national correspondent lender.

During the first decade of Christine working originations she made a splash winning branch sales contests and receiving the 1997 Affiliate of the Year award from her local chapter of Realtors (a voted-upon nomination amongst dozens of other candidates). She moved on in her career to management while dedicating much time to community work, which she still does today, having formed her own foundation, The Charles Brown Memorial Scholarship in the memory of a lifelong friend.

In 2002, Christine received an International Award from her then employer, H & R Block, for community contributions and her image as VP of Sales for the mortgage division of Block, also a peer nominated award chosen from thousands of employees as the single honoree for that year.

Over the last two decades, Christine has gone on to win countless national sales awards, proving that time and market changes, company, and contest metric changes cannot stop her from reaching the top of any sales chain.

She has also developed herself as a sought after public speaker on finance and real estate expert panels and lectures. Today she owns her own company *20/20 Vision For Success*, www.visionyoursuccess.net, a private coaching and seminar company through which Christine consults with businesses, youth programs, and sales teams on the traits and tricks of *Seeing your way to Success.*

While Christine has always been an elite female sales person, breaking her first glass ceiling in 2003, she was officially published as one of the Top 50 Elite Women in Mortgage in America by MPA (Mortgage Professionals of America) magazine. She would repeat that in 2017 in an even harder competitive race with a resurgence of mortgage professionals and was featured on the very first page of MPA Elite Women again. This recognition is not a paid for advertisement, rather it is a nominated competition for all women in the industry that is vetted, and both professionally and publicly culled to the most elite women. Christine takes pride in having been welcomed twice into the ranks of ground breaking women in the industry who have forever changed the face of this industry.

In March of 2018 Christine will be featured on the cover of Women's Mortgage Magazine, in the spot light at a time when women leadership is profoundly needed. And as we put the finishing touches on this book she is reaching new heights in her speaking career having been one of the key speakers at several national conventions.

Christine has long dreamed of becoming an Author and second to having her son says, "this is one of the greatest moments of my life". Christine's future plans include continuing to manage the sales at her current full-time employment while growing her personal company and contributions to communities and individuals seeking guidance and direction both in life and their professions.

Christine enjoys keeping her home, cooking, spending time with her family and boyfriend, and riding her Harley Davidson on weekends. She loves gardening and most of all her greatest joy comes from coaching and writing.

What Our Readers Say...

"If you're looking for a roadmap to success in life or your career, this book can easily serve as your bible. Christine speaks candidly and from the heart throughout this book. In doing so, she turns the many lessons from her life and career into a meaningful roadmap to success for others to follow."

~ Joseph Panebianco, CEO
AnnieMac Home Mortgage

"Christine takes her readers through a process of self-discovery to confront their fears and address the core of what is required in their business and personal life to make meaningful change. Every page is packed with practical, step-ty-step guidance, making it extremely clear and simple to reach new levels of success. This is a powerful book for any professional, and I'm excited for the many lives this will change as a result.

~ Kristin Messerli, Founder, Cultural Outreach Solutions
Managing Editor: Mortgage Women Magazine

"Christine is one of the few leaders in the Mortgage Industry. She is open, raw, real and authentic. This book takes away fluff and shares all that she has seen in creating success; not only for herself but for others. If you desire a step-by-step process to create success for yourself this is your book, especially for mortgage professionals! Start reading today and guaranteed you will find golden nuggets."

~Jessica Peterson, Best Selling Author

Founder Simply WOW Agency

"*Christine Beckwith has been one of the most influential people in the financial industry; she has shown me by her example how to navigate a woman's role in an often man dominated business world. She has demonstrated how to operate with grace, dignity and remain steadfast. She has shown many women in business that you can hold steady to conviction and you can proceed with class and diplomacy. Her book Wise Eyes shows us all how to sharpen our Vision for Success and gives three very practical application phases for this development. Since my read, I have found myself assessing my journey from vision to action and my mindset. Not a day goes by that I fail to apply a lesson from one of eight CORE philosophies of success. Thank you, Christine, for being a real-world role model and for committing to share your vision for our success.*

~ Kerry Fitzpatrick, Co-Founder, Associate Worx

"*Christine's book is a wonderful tribute to her spirit and character. She did not allow painful experiences to define who she is, instead using them as a source of wisdom, encouragement, and strength to overcome the trials and tribulations in her past and be an inspiration for others to follow. Through her success in life she remains true to who she really is.*"

~ Jutka Varhegyi, Licensed Clinical Counselor

Affirmations ~ Thoughts

Journal your way to mental freedom. Take ten steps and be in control rather than controlled.

Eighty percent of your sale is in the simple step of asking for the business.

Achieving a dream is about more than what you accomplish. It's about who you become in the process!

Successful sales people analyze and then jump into action.

Consistent and measurable growth is not out of mortgage professionals control! It's all in their mindset and ability to adapt.

To dream is to allow oneself the ability to transcend to a better place, to imagine a better future. To then chase those dreams with a genuine belief that they can become a reality takes courage, strength, endurance, and some strategic ignorance. Lucky for me that is how I was born.

Top sales people gain vast wealth by driving hard to daily best practices. Top sales people know where to look.

Growth cannot occur in the dark. First you must water yourself regularly and place yourself in the sunlight. No farmer ever grew a crop in the shade without water.

Have Faith, Be Strong, Believe

Made in the USA
Lexington, KY
10 September 2018